P9-BXZ-290

Connecticut
Agriculture in the Classroom
A
Literary
Gift
from CTAEF
visit us at
ctaef.org
CONNECTICUT AGRICULTURAL · EDUCATION FOUNDATION ·

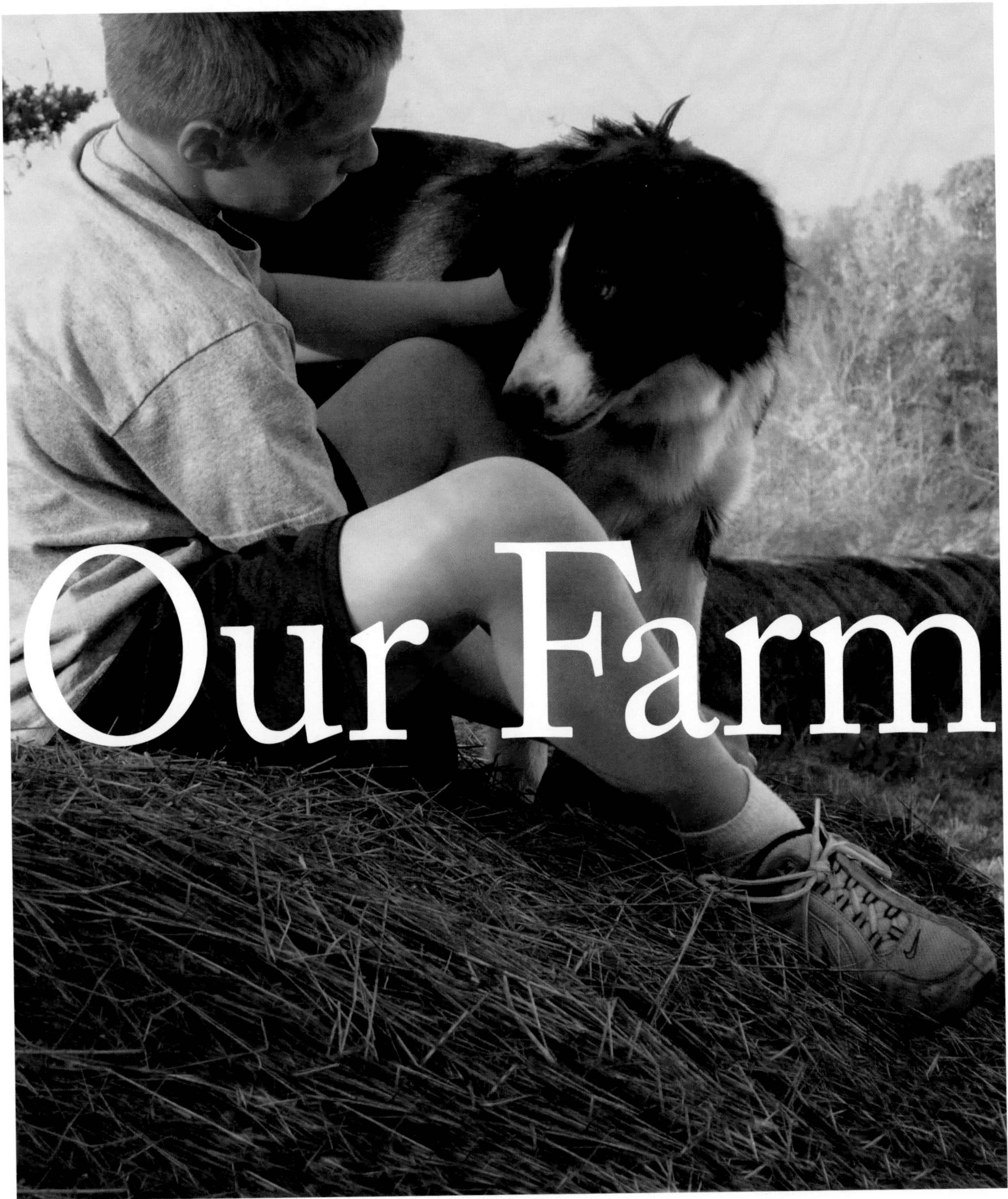
Our Farm

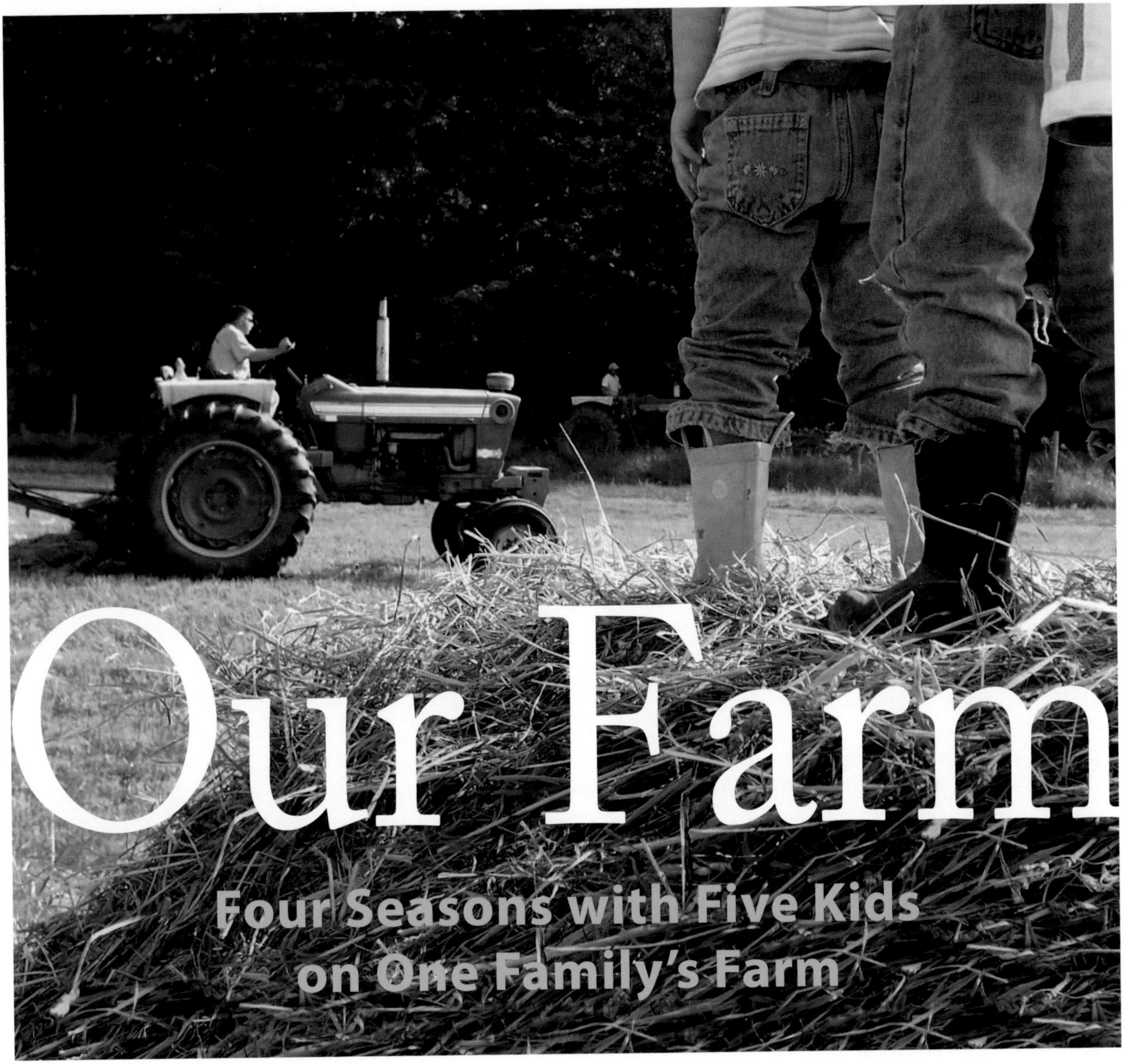

# Our Farm

## Four Seasons with Five Kids on One Family's Farm

written and photographed by Michael J. Rosen

Design by Gregory Hischak

Rosen, Michael J., 1954–
Our farm: four seasons with five kids on one family's farm / Michael J. Rosen, with photographs by the author.
p. ; cm.
ISBN 978-1-58196-067-9

Ages 10 and up.—Summary: A journal of one year on the Bennett farm in central Ohio. Shows how one family, with the help of relatives and friends, creates a life and livelihood on a 150-acre farm.

1. Farm life—Ohio—Juvenile literature. 2. Farms—Ohio—Juvenile literature. [1. Farm life—Ohio. 2. Farms—Ohio.]
I. Title. II. Author.
S521.5.O3 R67 2008
630/.9771/59 dc22
OCLC: 209910204

Darby Creek Publishing
7858 Industrial Parkway, Plain City, OH 43064
www.darbycreekpublishing.com



Printed in the United States of America
2 - BP - 1/1/2010

# Contents

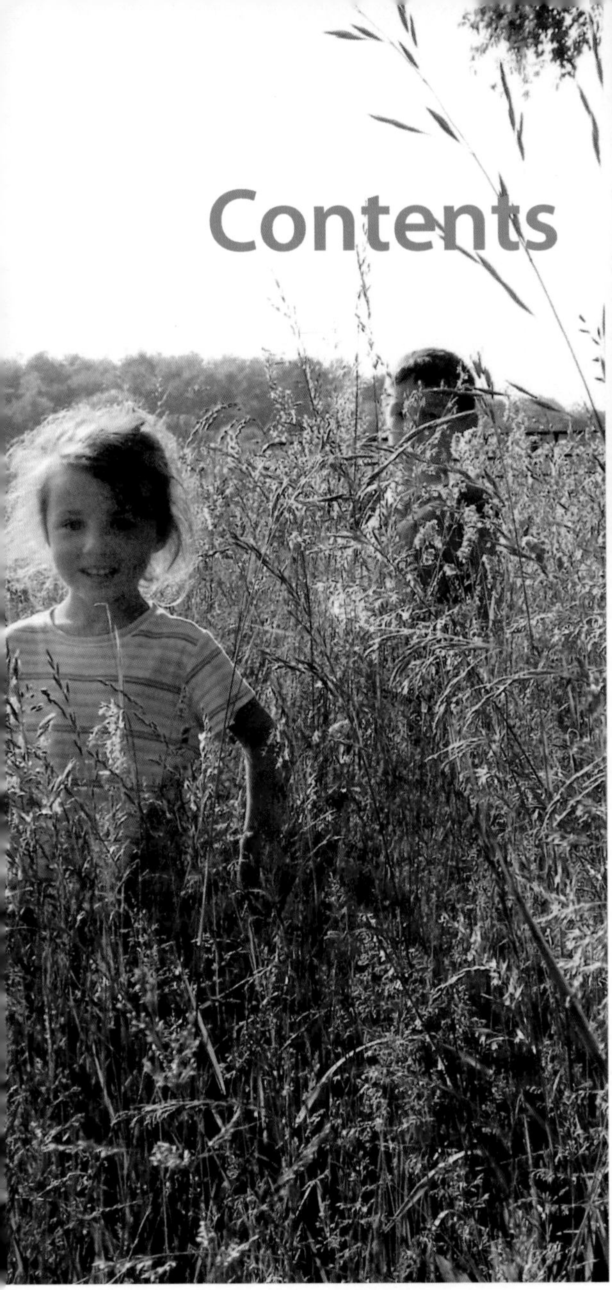

# A Note from the Author

*Our Farm* does not depict a "typical" farm—whatever that is. This one-year journal of the Bennett farm suggests neither a new "back-to-Earth" vision nor a nostalgic model of country life. Their farm is simply the way that one particular family, with the help of relatives and friends, creates a life and livelihood on a 150-acre plot of our shared planet.

The Bennetts live in a thinly populated part of central Ohio in the foothills of the Appalachian Mountains. Their home is just outside the village of Glenford in Perry County, founded in 1817.

The Bennett farm, unlike many depicted in nonfiction books about farming, is not grand, newly painted, bordered with flower gardens, and populated with a picture-perfect cast of characters: "Granny" with her windowsill of freshly baked pies and a new apron she sewed herself; "Pappy" tinkering with the broken tiller at the crack of dawn; "Baby Lily" making clover necklaces while "Daddy" waves from his bright green tractor. No, this is an authentic family as rushed and relaxed, as serious and silly, as hopeful and exhausted as your own family at any moment in time.

But looking at their farm should reveal the idea of farming and rural life anywhere in the United States, even as families in Florida, California, or Texas might be tending avocadoes or artichokes rather than this Ohio family's alfalfa and Angus cattle.

Today three-quarters of all the land in this country—2,052 out of the 3,142 counties—and one-fifth of all people in the United States, live in rural areas much like the Bennetts' acres. The term "rural," which can include both "farm" and "nonfarm" properties, specifically describes communities smaller than 2,500 people; it's usually thought of as the opposite of denser urban or metropolitan communities.

*Our Farm* is a photographic journal set in four seasons on the Bennett farm. My own commentary is intentionally brief. Generously welcomed into their home to photograph the daily activities and minor events, I primarily guided our conversations with questions—the sort of questions I imagined young readers might pose. The responses, in keeping, are primarily from the five Bennett children—after all, *Our Farm* belongs to them.

# Our Farm

## by the Numbers

**5 children** are in the Bennett family

**31 cows** compose the present herd (29 cows and 2 bulls)

**2 hens** occupy the barn—no longer laying eggs in the coop

**2 or 3 (there may be more) cats** hide out in the hayloft

**5 families** live within a 1-mile radius of the Bennett farm

**20 relatives** live within a 15-minute drive

**35,246 people** reside in Perry County, Ohio

**30,347 people** who reside in Perry County were born there

**86 people** occupy each square mile of Perry County (on average)

**277 people** occupy each square mile of Ohio (on average)

**1,138 people** occupy each square mile (on average) of New Jersey, the densest state

**200 people** reside in the town of Glenford, Ohio (the population hasn't changed much in decades)

**114 acres** compose the average farm in Perry County

**149.79 acres** compose the Bennett farm

**75 acres** of the Bennett farm are "mowed" either by machines or cows (the other half are buildings, roads, water, forest, or steeper fields)

**92.33 percent** of the farms in Perry County are family-owned

**1844** is the year that the main house on the farm was originally built

**16,027 acres** of corn (for grain) are planted in the county

**2,099 acres** of wheat are planted in the county

**12,089 acres** of soybeans are planted in the county

# Welcome

The Bennetts raise cows (primarily to sell their calves), grow all the alfalfa needed for their herd, and—depending on the year—raise chickens and tend a vegetable garden to provide food for their own meals.

Most years, they've also saved money to undertake a new project: replacement windows for their old farm house; digging a pond to stock with "good eating" fish; clearing a field for a small orchard; adding a deck and outdoor picnic table outside the kitchen. On top of all that, the Bennetts raise five children (four of whom attend local schools and one four-year-old who learns at home with Mom); co-own and work at the local plumbing company/hardware supply; and help the other members of their extended family keep their oil wells running, furnaces firing, and tractors operating. This cooperative spirit is at the heart of community life.

## The Family

### Caleb

**Age 17**

Anything that needs done is what I do—tractors, mowing, cows. When I get home from school, Dad usually has a job for me. Aside from that, I play varsity football, wrestling, and baseball—I've been the scholar athlete for my class every year. I also coach my brothers, Cayne and Grey, in wrestling and baseball. When I don't have my own practices, I coach them, either as the official team coach or just to help them fix whatever problems they're having. And that playing field right outside the house? That's where I spend most of my time if I'm not working. Otherwise, I drive to school and back, and that's about it. I just don't want to drive that much—I'm in the driver's seat of a tractor or a Bobcat so much, the idea of driving is already pretty old.

For college, I thought about pursuing nursing—male nurses are really in demand—but I'm leaning toward accounting now, since I'm good with math. It would be nice to stay and live here—but a recent hunting trip with my dad made me think I'd really like to get some land out in South Dakota; it's beautiful out there. Or I'd go wherever a job takes me.

## Chase

**Age 15**

If you come over about 9:30 any night, you'd find me in my bed reading—it's my favorite thing. Reading and working with the cows, those are my two things around here. This spring, I was working really hard, keeping the cows maintained before and after school, and keeping straight As. So as a reward, Dad bought us kids an Xbox. It's sort of funny that I'm the least video-game person in the family. I enjoy games like Risk and chess that Mom and I play. We also watch the History and Discovery channels. (If we're watching TV, someone will always say, "That's boring," and hope we'll change the channel.)

I'm pretty good at cooking—and I babysit for free, which my parents really like. Since seventh grade, I've been pretty science and mathematics oriented, so I'm thinking of engineering one day, maybe. My dream? That would be to work at NASA as a scientist.

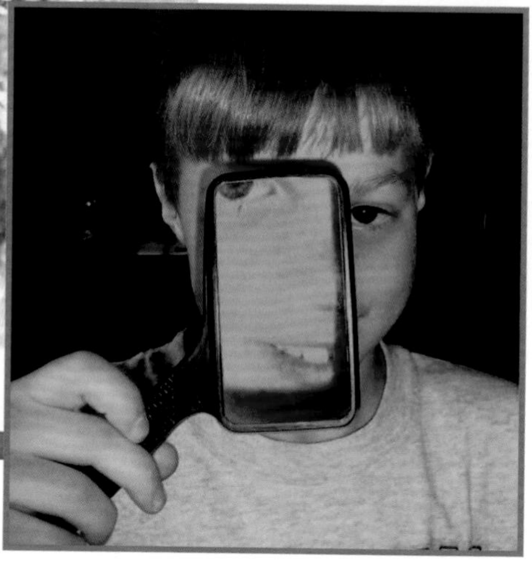

# Cayne

**Age 10**

I really think working around the farm is fun. After farm work, my favorite things are backyard football and baseball or swimming in the pond. Then reading would be my favorite school subject—and bacon cheeseburger pasta would be my favorite food. I also like deer tenderloin when we cook it outside on a fire. Sheridan High School is my favorite team, and after that, Ohio State and Texas for football. (You can probably tell because a lot of my clothes have the Sheridan logo.) When I'm twenty-five, I guess I'll be a builder, I think, because I like to work with a hammer and nails, and I'll live somewhere in Ohio —somewhere in the country, where it's quiet.

## Grey

**Age 8**

It's rough, I can tell you, being the youngest of the four boys. With all brothers that are older, I get in a lot of fights. But when we play football, I'm the littlest, and still, sometimes I smoke Cayne because I'm really fast. Baseball is my favorite sport so far. I play shortstop and second base, and sometimes first; I made all-stars in the Glenford Youth Organization. And I'm a good wrestler, too.

Cayne and I are in charge of the chickens and the dogs. The tree house is really my idea; I built most of it with Mom one day, and then everyone wanted to join in. When we tore up the house, I worked with Melvin sometimes, like on days off from school and then during the summer. I was great at the demolition part and helping do the drywall. I like the *Myth Busters* TV show, games on the Internet, corn on the cob, and catching fish—especially the ones Caleb catches, since he doesn't eat them. More for me!

# Ali

**Age 4**

My favorite thing is that I can wear dirty clothes on the farm. (They're more comfortable, but Mom doesn't let us wear our farm clothes to town.) Going on vacation is great, too, like when we went on an inner tube and got pulled by a boat in Deep Creek Lake, Maryland.

The best thing about having four brothers is nothing. The only nice thing they let me do is run for touchdowns when we play football. But, like if I say, "Be still and quit wiggling!" they'll just yell and wiggle.

I love our swing set, playing ball where you don't have to wonder if it's going to roll into the street where you can't go get it, bike riding, playing in the hayloft, going crawdad hunting, and fishing right outside. (Cayne caught an awesome fish once with huge teeth, and he couldn't even hold it, it was so spiny.) I like feeding the chickens—that's fun. My favorite chicken is Oddball; I gave him his name, and he's funny looking.

I'll probably be a mom when I grow up. I'll have a farm, I'll grow corn, definitely—plus broccoli, have lots of dogs and cats, and I'll have four girls and only one boy.

## Mom (Becky Bennett)

I grew up on thirty-five acres in this county. We had a pond, a forest, a barn, chickens, and a donkey—but it wasn't a working farm. We tended a garden. We canned and made pies. And if Mom left for an evening, my dad, sister, and I would pick a big, big bouquet of wildflowers to surprise her when she came home.

So I always knew I wanted to live in the country, and, except for one year I spent in business school in Columbus, I've lived in the county where I was born. While I was living in the city, I thought, "What is the point of having a balcony in this apartment if all you look at is concrete and cars?" And there was nowhere you could be alone; there were people anywhere you walked.

I gave up accounting as soon as I had my first child: I wanted to be here with my kids. Still, I had no idea of living on a real farm.

It's different having four boys; boys just roll with the punches. (I was raised with two sisters—girls are moodier and grouchier and not just over-and-gone so fast.) Now my kids are going to the same elementary school that their dad did; Caleb's and Chase's kindergarten teacher was his teacher, too. And all the kids are going—or will go—to the same middle and high school that their dad and I attended. That's where we met, all those years ago.

## Dad (Dave Bennett)

I was born and raised in Perry County, and I'm raising my family here. My father was a twenty-two-year military man, and he didn't hunt, fish, or play sports (all the things I do now). But when I was twelve, I made a life-long association with a longtime farmer, John Campbell. He was about sixty-five when I met him. John really taught me everything I know about farming: beef, sheep, hogs, and baling. He had no children, so it was the two of us. I'd meet him at eight in the morning; we'd feed the animals, we'd go down to the "loafing station" in Glenford where all the farmers would talk about weather and livestock, then we'd go back and mow or bale, and then we'd do the evening feeding. A whole different way of life back then.

That was in the 1970s, before and after school, and even during school hours when it was corn, wheat, or oat harvesting.

Now I work this farm with the Davy family. And I'm one of the original owners of the county's largest hardware/plumbing business.

There is an old saying: "It's a good thing for the American public that farming is a disease, not an occupation." If you relied on farming to make money, you'd never do it. But when you grow up doing it, you have this desire to work with cattle or to grow crops, or to do whatever it is. I could spend the time I spend farming doing something else and make more money, but I can't stop farming. So I make my living plumbing, and we live our lives farming.

# The Dogs

The Bennett family has always included dogs—working dogs, mostly. Simon hunts coons, Angus herds cattle, and Bo, the three-legged beagle, divides his time between hunting rabbits and being a companion animal for the younger children.

"Cayne and I get paid," Grey says, "not very often, but a little bit, to take care of the dogs' food and water, although the dogs on the porch usually like to drink from the pond. And we give them straw in their doghouses to keep them warm—a lot of straw in the winter, and they pack it down and make a cozy den in their houses."

Since the Bennett house is far from the road (and it's a nearly traffic-less county road at that), and since it has no fenced-in yard similar to those that might confine a city dog, the Bennett dogs enjoy most days without the city's need for leashes or the indoor's need for more training and calm behavior. They roam the property, chase wildlife, wade into the water when it suits them, roll in mud or something dead, and pretty much enjoy what the great outdoors has to offer a dog.

A descendent of the English Foxhound, the Treeing Walker Coonhound is an energetic, trainable hound that's a fast runner, and a keen hunter. It uses its "bugle-like" voice when he's treed a varmint, but it is just as eager and able to climb the tree himself. The dog is named for Thomas Walker, who first brought the dog to Virginia in the 18th century, and for its ability to tree its quarry.

## Simon (Treeing Walker Coonhound)

**about 4 years old**

**Cayne:** Simon is a Treeing Walker Coonhound and we take him coon hunting. When he first picks up the scent, he gives a trail bark: a really long *au-oooooooooh* bark. And then, once he's treed the coon, his bark is real short and choppy, like *au-of, au-of, au-of.* When we hear that bark, we go find him and shine a big flashlight into the tree and look through the riflescope. If you see the coon, you take a shot with a .22 rifle. We take the raccoon home and give it to Cliff down the road. He skins coons and makes pelts.

**Chase:** No one eats raccoon, I don't think. We just hunt them for sport—but they're a real nuisance animal, too, because they tear up your garden, get in the trash, shred your lawn—that sort of thing. Now when I go out coon hunting with Simon, he likes to chase deer instead. You go out at dark, but if it's really bright, the coons won't be out. Now our woods aren't as good for hunting, because we've just logged our woods and the biggest trees are gone. But before, the coons could run up trees and across fallen logs, and there was a lot of underbrush and hollow logs to hide in. That throws a dog off.

One time, Simon and I tracked a coon clear across the pasture to the old house, which is just an abandoned building really with only half of a foundation. So this sly raccoon ran inside and hid. Well, I thought we'd lost it, and then Dad came back to see how we were doing. Simon was barking and scratching at the wall, and I was wondering, *What are you doing, dog?* Then Dad busted open the wall, and there was the coon—Simon was right. So we gave it to my Uncle Cliff; he sells pelts.

## Bo (Beagle) age 5

**Cayne:** One time, when Bo was only a few months old, he was out rabbit hunting on his own—we guess that's what happened—and this huge dog came along and bit his leg. And the vet had to take his leg off. So almost from the start, Bo had three legs.

**Mom:** Let's back up. We picked Bo out of a litter from a friend's house (he was about three months old) and shortly thereafter headed on a short vacation. Ryan, who was taking care of the animals while we were gone, couldn't find Bo one day. And when we came back, we heard that some people had found a hurt beagle puppy, so Dad and the older boys went over.

**Chase:** Yes, they were keeping Bo safe, tied to a box, with water and food, but his leg was just dangling there. So I wrapped him in a towel, and Dad drove Bo and Caleb and me to the vet's office. On the way over, Dad said, "You know, Bo isn't really a hunting dog yet, so if you and Caleb really want him and want to spend $350 out of your own pockets, then we'll let the vet try to fix his leg." We really wanted to save Bo. When we got Bo home, Dad said, "Okay, I'll pay you boys back the money."

**Dad:** I paid $25 for Bo, so paying the vet all that money for a young dog—well, I wanted to be sure that the boys really wanted that dog and were going to care for him. It's easy to say "yes" with Dad's money, but with your own?

**Chase:** The doctor had to take off Bo's leg and stitch him up. Then Bo had to wear a cone on his head for a while. But he recovered and he got used to having just three legs. Now he doesn't even know he's missing a leg. And the amazing thing is, he is a great rabbit hunter.

**Grey:** Bo makes me kind of sad for him because his leg is gone, but he goes everywhere he wants to go and runs really fast on three legs. He likes to play with the other dogs. Like Bo and Angus will play-fight, and Bo runs a big circle around Angus and then does this football hit right at him.

Angus locates a new calf among the bramble and trees that border the creek. Mother cows often hide or move far from the other animals when delivering.

## Angus (Border Collie) age 4

**Grey:** If my dad wants the cows to run into one gate or a different gate, Angus understands and makes them move. That's why Angus is here. The cows are afraid of him, even though they sometimes charge him. He runs at their ankles, and that makes them move on. Angus also wants to herd everything else: cats, chickens, the other dogs, machines—anything that moves.

**Chase:** I just enjoy working with the cows. I guess you have to if you're going to spend that much time with them. Angus spends even more time.

There was this cow, and she was due for a calf, and I had to check her every day for about week. I was the guy on the walkie-talkie calling my dad, and he'd say, "Yep, Chase, sounds like you'd better check her every fifteen or twenty minutes." So it just sort of happened that every spring I became the guy who would check all the cows. With Angus, of course. So don't ask me how, but if a cow is missing, I just say, "Where's the cow, Angus?" or "Where's the calf?" and he knows! I follow him, and there she'd be. Especially during calving time, Angus always knows when a cow needs us. He spends all his time with the cows, so he just knows.

**Grey:** If there were a challenge for who can bring the cows in—without having any training or practice—Angus would win. He is the greatest dog ever at watching cows. He sticks his ears up and crouches down and just watches them, looks at them and sees what they are doing. (Mostly they are just standing there!) He looks at a cow in a way that's a lot different from the way he looks at people.

**Chase:** There's this one cow, one of the red cows, and Angus was trying to move it, and the cow just charged him. Angus took a couple of good licks—that red cow pretty much ran over him—but he didn't get hurt. I guess that's part of what Angus knows, too—how to get around the cows carefully.

**Dad:** Training? He trained himself! Day after day, he assists us with the cattle. He figured out his way of helping just by doing it every day. I'd just connect a word with the action he was already doing out of natural instincts. He knows: "Where are the cows at?" and "Where are the calves at?" (Those are two different things.) Whatever I ask, he takes me right to the animals.

**Mom:** When Dave's not in the barn, Angus is. That's his life. We always take Angus inside when it's really cold. But by two or three in the morning, he's waking us up, whining and pacing—wanting to go out. He just knows there might be something going on with his cows. So we let him out.

## Cats

**The loft provides an almost infinite number of hiding places for the resident cats.**

**Chase:** We feed and water the cats up in the hayloft, too, although they find their own food. The cats are scared of us, but if they're really hungry, they'll come over if we have some food. Then, suddenly, they forget they're afraid.

**Cayne:** The cats found us, really. They came from my grandma. They just showed up on her porch, and she gave them to us. So we always make sure they have food during the winter, and we put some out the rest of the year when they're fending for themselves on mice, which is what we're glad they eat—and birds and rabbits, too, which we're not as glad about.

**Grey:** We call the orange one "Tiger," but there are three or four more, and we don't have names for them. We hardly see them up close very much. Mostly it's their glowing eyes from among the hay bales. Only one of them will let me pick it up. For sure, they will never come if you call them.

# The Farm

**Along the winding road that leads to the Bennett farm, you'll find a stream, but no fire hydrants. If ever a fire broke out, the volunteer firefighters would pump water from the new pond through their hoses.**

**Dad:** When Mom and I met, we still lived next door to my friend and mentor, John Campbell. When we had Caleb, John and Betty would care for him like he was their grandchild. We rented this place starting in 1991 and then bought it in 1993. There were a lot of old, small buildings, plus two houses—one that was only semi-sound that we eventually let go. (The cows started to walk in and they'd break through the floor, so that meant we had to raze it.) We knocked down all the other buildings, except for the chicken coop and the double-sized corn shed, for safety reasons.

Eventually, we built a new barn for the cattle and a new shed. There is always something to build (and then to rebuild). You just count on that living out here: doing most things yourself or with a neighbor or with your kids as they grow bigger and stronger. Finally, we waited twelve years to add onto the house. We had the woods timbered and made the money needed to do the addition and all the remodeling.

**Dad: You can just barely make out the numbers on this board: 1844. We sort of built up around the original farmhouse, but this old board is still part of the basement.**

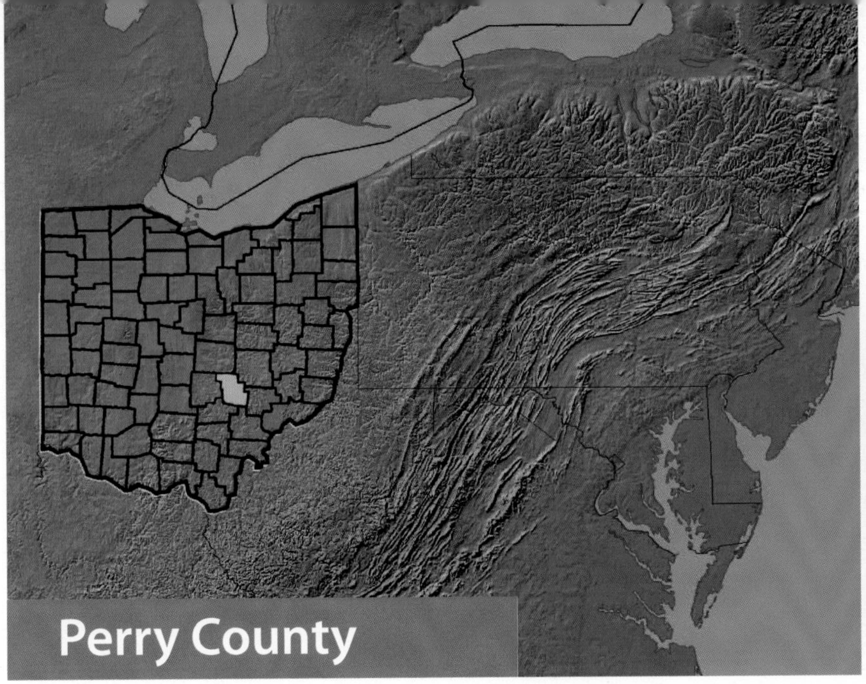

Of Ohio's twenty-nine Appalachian counties, Perry County is among the lowest in terms of household income. The county has no hospital, shopping mall, or major industry. (There are small healthcare facilities, shopping strip centers, and college branches within a twenty-five mile radius, although rural roads and road conditions often require longer travel time.) Local or aerial maps show: one park, one attraction (Dawes Arboretum), two libraries, and thirty-eight cemeteries.

There is no public transportation. About 80 percent of the residents drive to work, traveling an average of thirty-three minutes one way. Ten minutes from Glenford, two neighboring towns offer small libraries.

Columbus, some forty-five minutes away by car, does provide a wealth of cultural resources. Says Caleb, "I don't go except when our whole family goes, once in a while. It's too far, too crowded, and too expensive."

**Ali:** Our town is littler even than other little towns. All we have is one post office, one drive-through, Jeff's (where people get their cars fixed), and then Steve's, that's Swinehart's General Store, where we get one or two things if we run out.

**Chase:** We just got carryout pizza at the drive-through, and that's a first! And now there are two fast-food places: a Subway and a Taco Bell, about ten miles away in Thornport and Somerset. For a doctor, if you have anything that needs a specialist, we drive to Columbus.

**Cayne:** But Glenford is famous for one thing. We were state basketball champs in 1941. Out of the entire state. We're still known for that.

# Winter

## by the Numbers

**25 chicks**—quantity of chicks mail-ordered for the empty coop

**21 days**—length of time before an egg hatches into a chick (the incubation period)

**95°F**—temperature a chick must be kept for its first week (As it grows feathers, the high temperature is not as crucial.)

**5 to 11 years**—the natural lifespan of a chicken (differs from breed to breed)

**6 weeks**—the entire lifespan of a chicken grown for meat

**26 cows**—number of pregnant cows that will calve in the coming months

**12 cows**—number of pregnant cows fertilized by mail-ordered bull semen

**275 breeds**—approximate number of kinds of beef cattle raised throughout the world

**1/2 ton (1,000 pounds)**—weight of one round bale of hay

**70 pounds**—weight of one square bale of hay

**25 to 35 pounds**—amount of hay eaten by each cow in one day

**65 pounds**—amount of manure produced by each cow in one day (That's nearly twelve tons in a year, just for a single cow.)

**7 days**—number of snow days this year (No school!)

**53 miles**—length of high-tensile fencing that surrounds the Bennett pastures (Each fence has five wires, two of which carry an electrical charge.)

**43 miles**—distance from the Bennett farm to Columbus, Ohio, the nearest major city

# An Empty Coop

**Many families in the country, even those who don't consider themselves farmers, keep a few chickens. They aren't expensive to purchase, feed, or house. They don't require as much space or daily care as other livestock. And every twenty-four hours, they provide a new clutch of fresh eggs.**

**Grey:** We had nine chickens last year. (We had even more the year before that.) They liked to climb up or fly up on the ladder and roost. Not being on the ground makes them feel safer from predators. Two are roosters—one is red and one is white—and they are mean. All seven hens died while we were on vacation. Our cousin Ryan was taking care of the chickens, and just four possums ate seven chickens.

**Chase:** I found them. I went down to feed the chickens when we got back, and one possum was still there. It had climbed the wall and was standing on a beam, hissing down at me. Ryan told us he had put down live traps, and he had already caught three possums—they had been living under the coop.

**Mom:** I told Ryan that we really appreciated his help, especially for cleaning up the mess, but he said there was nothing to clean up. The possums had eaten the beaks, the feet, everything but the feathers. Even I thought that was gross!

**Cayne:** When we had thirteen layers—those are just hens bred to be good egg-layers—we could usually collect ten eggs from the coop each day when the hens were younger. But now, all of sudden, with only two mean roosters and no eggs, we have to start over with new chicks. We're going to build a new coop with a concrete floor so possums can't burrow in.

# Chicks

A fertilized chicken egg takes twenty-one days to hatch. Most commercial farmers use an incubator to keep steady warmth on the eggs, freeing up their hens to lay more eggs. (A chicken is an indeterminate layer, which is a bird that will continue to lay eggs until the nest contains a certain number of them—about a dozen in the case of chickens). If an egg is removed from the nest, it will lay another egg the following day. If a chicken were like a crow, a determinate layer, it would only lay a certain number of eggs during a season—and no more—regardless of each egg's fate.

While many farms do raise their own chicks or acquire them from neighbors, the Bennetts acquired their new flock from a farm in Iowa that ships chicks through the mail.

**Mom:** We ordered twenty-four chicks, but the company always sends you one more chick—an exotic one—for free. (I guess that's so you can see how beautiful it is so you'll order more of that kind the next year.) It cost us about fifty dollars for the chicks, and that included a kit with medicine to help them thrive. So the birds are maybe two dollars each.

**Cayne:** Last year, the exotic one we got was small, and it didn't live—and we lost six other chicks, as well. We never know exactly why. They're just tiny chicks and if one gets weak or sick, the others will peck it to death.

**Chase:** How about these names, Ali? Buff Orpington! Blue Andalusian! Fancy Top Hat Special! For a while, we had those Barred Rocks and those Rose Comb Brown Leghorns.

**Ali:** That one looks like he has a pillow on his head.

**Chase:** That's the White Crested Black Polish.

## Keeping Warm

On the Sunday before Valentine's Day, Mom, Ali, and Chase drive about thirty minutes to the larger post office in Zanesville. They could have waited a day, and the box of new chicks, sent from Iowa, could have been delivered to their local post office for a Monday pick-up, but Mom was worried about the chicks getting cold.

"A chill can kill a chick," she explains again to Ali, who wants to be the first to peek inside the box. "And you can't touch them, either," Mom reminds everyone. "Even though they're soft and little, you can't handle them yet. Promise?"

**Ali:** I didn't touch them, but I talked to the chicks through the holes in the box on the whole way home.

**Cayne:** We just opened up the box they came in inside this really large cardboard box we filled with some straw. Right way, the chicks all huddled under the lamp to keep warm. It's just a regular light bulb, but it makes enough heat. It's their sun.

**Mom:** If you accidentally put the lamp too close, the chicks will still stay right underneath anyway, and they'll get cooked! They don't know any better. It's amazing any of these birds live. By late spring, the birds will be big enough to live outside in the coop. But for now, their home is the cardboard box on the treadmill in the living room. So much for my exercising.

**Grey:** They run from one side of the box to the other when you try to pick them up. They're scared. They always sleep under the light, and we have to keep moving it up higher as they grow taller. If you surprise the chicks at night, they'll all be under the light, and then they all run to different parts as soon as they see you.

**Cayne:** When they're tiny you can't tell who's a male and who's a female. When they're older, the males start growing the wattle and the comb on the top of their heads. And that's how you know.

**Dad:** The chicks will be laying eggs this first year, but they won't know how to sit on them. Only a chick that's been sat on will sit. Don't ask me why. The chicks we bought were hatched in an incubator — that's a machine, not a mother hen—so they won't know how to brood at first. But we take the eggs before the hens really sit on them. We don't leave the eggs in the coop long enough for them to learn. If we wanted to hatch eggs to get more chicks, then the older hens that have laid eggs before would brood those eggs.

# Chick Economics

**Caleb:** This time we ordered the bigger, yellow chickens for meat and the black chickens for laying eggs. In six weeks, the yellow ones will be so big that they'll hardly be able to stand.

**Dad:** If you're raising just a few chickens for meat, it's certainly cheaper to buy what's already in packages at the store, if you know what I mean.

**Caleb:** A fifty-pound bag of their food—it's called laying mash—costs about seven dollars, and it lasts about two weeks for a dozen chickens. I can't give you a dollar figure for the time we put in caring for the chicks, but if we were selling them, that would be a factor.

**Dad:** But these chickens are ours. We'll know their lives and what they were fed. And they'll be tastier—I know it. But even more, Mom and I think it's a neat experience for the kids to raise the birds. We've only kept egg-layers before. So we'll see how it goes.

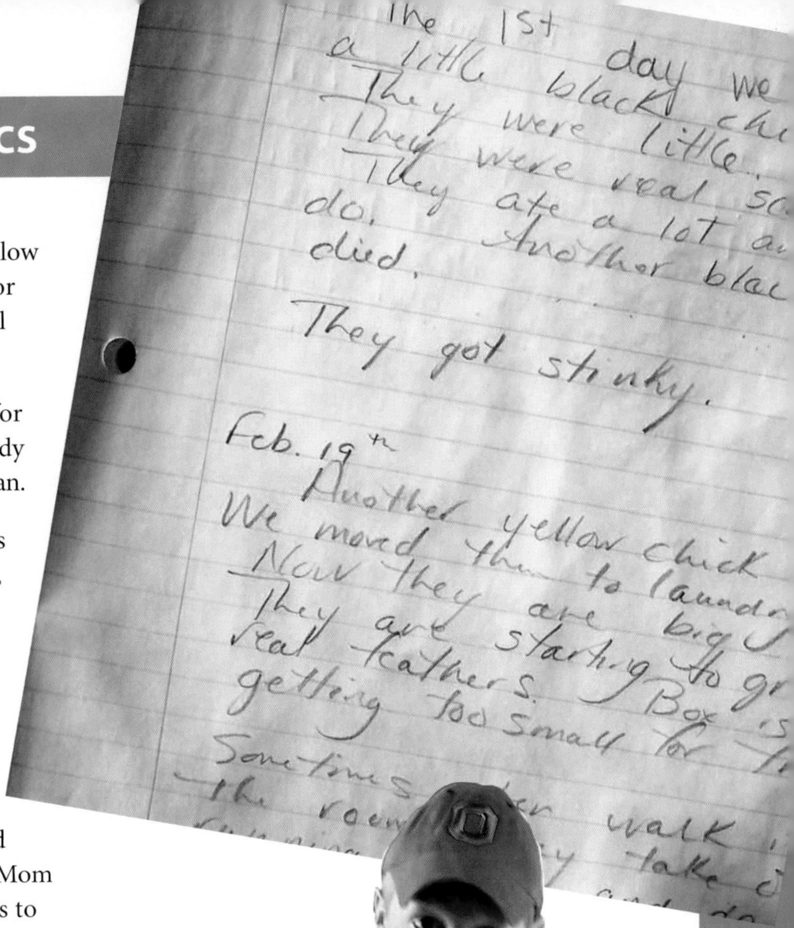

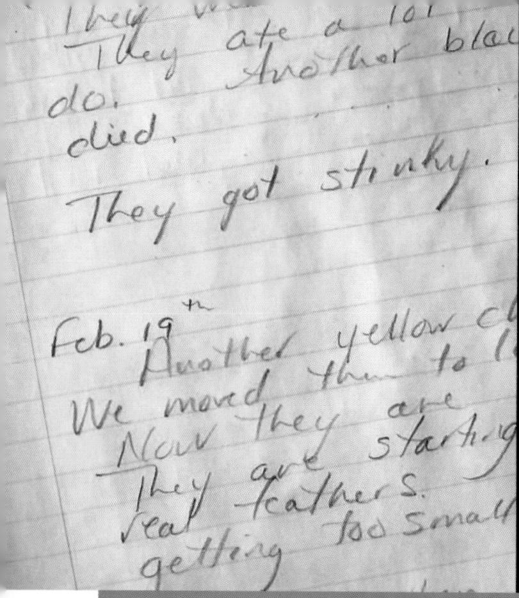

# Chicks Move to the Coop

**Grey:** After about ten days, we had to move the chicks into the laundry room. They sort of stunk up the living room. Poop. Even though we kept changing their straw. The chicks don't pick one spot—they just sort of go wherever—so we shove all the straw out with a big shovel and put in new straw. Down in the basement they can have their own area. In a couple of weeks, it will be warm enough to move them out to the coop. If the chicks get cold, they huddle up together under the light bulb.

**Caleb:** There is no talking about raising animals without talking about both ends of the animal. You're always feeding the one end, and you're always removing what comes out the other end. While it's rarely dinner-table conversation, the topic of feces—chickens', cows', dogs'—is a regular part of farm life. For instance, each chick that is being raised for meat will live forty-seven days, and in that short time period, it will create two pounds of litter (manure, with some wood shavings).

**Chase:** Once they're outside, we'll put a heater in the coop if it's really cold. But the building protects them from the wind, and they have feathers and down and lots of straw in their boxes, even though chickens like to sleep in the rafters and it is colder up higher. For water, we have heated pans that we can plug in—or else we have to go down to the coop all the time to break up the ice in the water.

We used to have troughs that were nailed on the floor—they were feeders—but now we have these small water tanks with a ring at the bottom that's always filled with water.

**Cayne:** Along with the chicken feed, they'll get lots of scraps—carrot peelings, lettuce, bread crusts, corncobs, apples. Chickens will eat pretty much anything.

**Grey:** In the old coop, there was a back room, like a shed with a door, and we could keep their bags of food there. If it were in the same room as the chickens, they would get into it and eat too much. I think they grow bigger slowly, but Mom says they grow fast.

**Chase:** I think they poop more than eat!

**Cayne:** The chicks will eat from your hands if you just hold the grain down near them in your open hands. First, they are kind of skittish, but then they come and eat a little from your hands. And then they get used to seeing us, and they all come over to be fed that way, just crowding in to peck. Sometimes you can feel their beaks, like you are being pinched.

**Grey:** Yes, sometimes they will bite your finger, but it doesn't hurt—kind of tickles. Chickens are softer than you think. (Roosters are not as soft as the hens.)

To pick up a chicken, you grab one with both hands and hold it down with one hand and slide your other underneath to hold both legs. At first, they're kind of scared, so you have to hold gently but by both legs. A chicken's body is light and soft. If you ever have to carry one far, you turn her upside down and hold her feet—and they're calmer.

**Chase:** Chicks drink in a weird way. They stand over the water and then dip down with their beaks open and scoop up a little water. But then they have to tilt their heads back to make the water go down. They can't suck in water, so gravity has to get it to trickle down their throats. People say turkeys can drown in a rainstorm if they hold their heads and try to drink. But I just read that's a myth.

One time I went out to the chicken coop, and I unlatched the hook and then closed the door so none of the chickens could get out, but the hook dropped back in place. I was stuck in the room with a bunch of chickens, plus there are snakes in there, and tons of cobwebs and bones. I'm petrified of snakes and always have been. I was about ten. I started screaming for help, but the coop is pretty far from the house, so nobody heard me for a while.

## Snow

**Cayne:** The steep hills on our property are perfect for sledding. There doesn't have to be a lot of snow—just enough to cover the ground. But a few inches make sledding even better. My longest ride lasted about a minute, I think, down one hill, up another little hill, then back down toward the pond, and all the way across the pasture to the fence.

**Grey:** We have one huge hill. Sometimes we'll have a party in the snow and everyone will start out on a sled back at the fence and ride as far as we can down the hill and onto the pond. But then the pond is like a three-feet drop from the bank, so that's like a jump! And if Dad takes us out on the snowmobile, that ride's a whole lot faster. But it doesn't go on the pond.

**Ali:** I can sled all the way down part of the driveway. Then I just lie down on the sled, and the boys can pull me back up the hill so I can go again. Sledding at our house is better because we never sled onto someone else's property. But ice-skating is hard; every single time, I fall backwards.

**Cayne:** We maybe have seven snow days every year. Two or three years ago we had a Level 3 snow emergency. Snowplows couldn't get back onto the small roads like ours.

**Mom:** Snow is usually not a problem. It's not like we have to drive an hour, or even fifteen minutes, two and three times a day to get to wherever we need to be. We're mostly home except for school and taking the boys to meets and practices.

**Cayne:** We went ice fishing at a neighbor's pond, and I caught twenty-one fish at this one hole. You take this special saw, and it spins on the ice to make a hole about the size of a coffee can lid. Then you just use a jigging pole. It's not like regular fishing. You lay your pole on the ice, and when a fish tugs on it, you grab your pole and reel it in, because the fish aren't active—they're slow.

**Grey:** I can't wait to go ice fishing on our pond, but our fish are still too small. We have gone skating. The first time we made an ice rink on the pond, Dad used a drill to test how thick the ice was. Then Cayne and I used this big, flat shovel and swept off the snow so the pond was just smooth ice.

**Dad:** When I was a kid, I remember that winters around here used to be all about snow: lots of snow! And the snow spells seemed to last much longer. But today, there are maybe a few days for the kids to play in the snow or go skating or sledding.

Now, being the adult, I see winter's main challenge is keeping our heat. If we get a cold snap and the winds go above ten miles per hour, we'll lose our heat because we use our oil well for heating. It produces the natural gas for our furnace, and that's our only

source of heat. So if it goes down, we bundle up and go walk the gas lines—the pipes lay on top of the ground—listening for the hissing of a leak in the line.

**Chase:** We used to have a wood burner right in the living room. When it got really cold or when the heat went out, we'd take our sleeping bags and sleep right in front that stove. It would be so cold everywhere else in the house, but not in front of the wood burner. So we'd wear sweatshirts and ski caps and curl up in front of the glass window in the door of the wood burner.

My favorite part of winter is eating snow.

**Ali:** I like to eat snow, too. It tastes like homemade ice cream.

**Chase:** But I probably wouldn't do that in the city since there's more pollution and motorists and acid rain and chemicals and everything. You wouldn't know what's in the snow you're eating. But here, the snow just falls right down through the clean air among the trees.

**Cayne:** Hey, Chase, remember: Never eat yellow snow!

# Storing Hay

The pastures on the Bennett farm provide much of the cows' food during warmer months. But those same grasses need to be harvested and stored to provide food for the barn cows, as well as for the entire herd, during months when the pasture grasses are dormant or buried in snow.

While Caleb, Josh, and their fathers take on most of the hay baling, it's primarily Chase who feeds the barn cows with the loft's square bales. Larger round bales are hauled to the food pens each day to feed the outside cows.

**Chase:** When we stack up the hay bales, we have to be careful about how dry or wet they are. We need them to be dry—but not too dry, because that can make them catch fire too easily. But if they're too wet, they can heat up from all the humidity. The bacteria, I guess, gets the hay cooking inside—like making compost. You can put your hand on a bale, and it will feel hot, even though it's been sitting inside under a roof where it's pretty cool.

We can check the moisture in a few sample bales with this special meter. You stick this rod inside the bale, press a button, and it gives you a reading—fourteen percent and under is pretty good.

Used to be, you couldn't walk in the barn without seeing rats. So we set out live traps—rectangular cages—and if they stepped in to get the peanut-butter cracker, the cages would slam shut. But even after catching a few rats, we knew there were lots more, and they were eating all the corn we'd bought for the cows.

So this is what we did: At night, we shut off the lights in the barn and set down some grain by the grain feeder. Then we hid and waited, like five minutes, and then we hit the lights, and all these rats were surrounding the grain. We used BB guns to get rid of them. But some are always going to be around. The cats help.

# Hay and Hayloft

**Cayne:** The hayloft is where we store the square bales and where we have our clubhouse so we can raise the cows under it. You can't raise your animals above—that would be a lot of heavy animals over your head!

**Grey:** We always have a fort up in the hayloft, but then my dad feeds the bales to the cows, and the cows eventually eat the whole fort. And then we make a new one the next summer.

**Ali:** The boys help me make my fort in the hayloft. I can't lift the bales myself. I tell them where to put them, and then we put them back when we're done. But Dad gets mad if we drop bales off the edge, because the strings break off and the hay gets everywhere. And it's the cow's food!

**Grey:** To make the fort, you just move the hay bales and make tunnels and rooms—except they're pretty heavy, I think sixty or seventy pounds each, and I only weigh fifty pounds.

**Caleb:** If they were wet, Grey, you'd never be able to lift them. I bet they're almost twice the weight then. And the round bales, out in the field, they weigh more like 1,100 pounds. That's like twenty-two of you, Grey.

**Grey:** But you don't lift those either.

**Caleb:** Right, the skid steer does.

**Ali:** I weigh thirty-four pounds.

**Chase:** Okay, so two of you would make one square bale, Ali—and thirty-three of you would make one round bale. But then, the cows would have to eat you.

**Cayne:** Once, we even made this hotel out of hay bales up in the loft. It was so big, with lots of rooms and all, and you could stretch out and be really comfortable up there. It was awesome. And that's like a story my dad told us about when he was little: They had lots of square bales at Dad's older sister's house near where he grew up. She had a horse farm. Looking at the hayloft, everyone thought, "Yep, the horses have plenty of hay bales for the winter." But it was only huge on the outside. Inside, it was mostly hollow, where Dad had made himself a fort with lots of hollow spaces to crawl around in. So the family had to go out and buy other hay, and I guess Dad got into trouble.

# Knee Football and Other Games

**Chase:** We invented this game of knee football, which we played in the house in a small room, so the rule was that you couldn't run standing up. But then we broke something, and Mom said that was that. So Caleb and I decided we could play up in the hayloft. It was like forty degrees up there, but we set some hay bales on their sides all the way around the edge so no one could fall. There was a lot of loose hay and straw on the floor, so we could play tackle football up there for most of the winter.

**Grey:** The loft is also where we play sharks and minnows and football—and when Josh nailed a cardboard backboard up there, we had a hoop for playing basketball, but just with a little ball. And it's where we have hay fights, sometimes all five of us, plus Dylan and Josh. And when hay is falling down, sometimes a cow will stretch its head up and eat it.

**Chase:** Our biggest fights are when we get Caleb and Josh to play, so we have to get them mad first—and then we lose badly, real badly. One time we had a hay fight but with added water buckets. We filled buckets and placed them at every possible entrance around the hayloft, ready to dump them on the older boys as soon as they came in.

**Grey:** But then Josh took me as hostage and dunked me in the cow's drinking trough, which was so gross—and cold!

**Chase:** Yes, we got them the first time, but not after that. It wasn't pretty for us.

**Grey:** We also like to walk on the rafters in the barn. At first it's scary, but once you get used to it, you can walk without holding the bars. And if you drop, it's only maybe five feet—onto your feet.

**Cayne:** It's like walking the tightrope at a circus, but you have hay instead of a net to break your fall.

## Alfalfa

A round bale weighs about the same as twenty-two square bales. Being so large and heavy, the round bales stay outside, wrapped in plastic or bound in twine. To move a round bale, one of the older boys or Dad drives the skid steer with the hay spear in the front toward a bale, "harpoons" it, and then hauls it over to what looks like a small corral: a round-bale feeder that holds one bale and allows cows to feed around its entire perimeter. As Caleb says, "By the time I've snipped off the twine, the herd is right there eating."

Round bales line the frozen gravel driveway that runs past the barn toward the house. Others are stacked inside the barn or alongside the old double corncrib, adjacent to nearby alfalfa fields that the Bennetts harvested in three cuttings. The first mowing usually takes place about June 1st; the second, thirty days after that; and the last cutting, about sixty days later. Grasses grow more slowly in mid-summer when the soil is drier.

"We usually mow at night, so the grass stays moister and greener when you bale it," says Caleb, who mowed most of the fields along with his buddy, Josh. "That grassy-green taste is what the cows love."

**Grey:** When a bale smells bad, that means it tastes good to the cows.

**Caleb:** One round bale will feed our twenty-eight cows for one day. So we go through seven bales a week. When we get to June, we'll have twenty-eight cows and, we hope, twenty-eight calves, but all the calves eat is milk for a couple months and then a little grass, and then the calves get sold. By then, the calf is about three-fourths the size of the mother, and it will still be sucking milk from her.

**Dad:** One difference between our cows—which we're raising for meat—and dairy cows is that dairy cows don't get to graze. Since they have to produce milk all the time, they're milked, then they eat special high-protein food, then they lie down, and then they're milked again in the evening.

# Feed Time

**Chase:** The inside cows are either the ones we don't want the bull to accidentally breed with, or they are the ones we're feeding out. We keep maybe five or six cows inside and fatten them up with corn and hay. That gets them fat, and it's the fat that makes the tastiest meat. Or if we're just selling a calf, we want it to look healthier and more muscular so it sells for more, so we feed it more corn, too, along with the hay.

We don't grow corn. We go to Dennis or Ted's farm, and we buy it by the bushel. It's hard corn—not like the sweet corn people eat. Not at all. It's crunchy, dry, and full of dust from the grinding. But the cows really like it.

**Ideally, one of the Bennett cows being fed out before butchering should gain between two and three pounds per day.**

The best cow we have is part Maine and part Angus. She's #10, but we've only got three or four calves from her in about ten years because she's been sick a lot. We're not always sure why. The vet's given her antibiotics before—like when she got a disease from flies that made her tongue swell: she lost almost four hundred pounds before she felt well enough to eat.

So our cows eat all natural food. We do give them salt and certain minerals they need to stay well, but never anything like artificial stuff or growth hormones. And we don't use pesticides and herbicides on the pastures. So our cows are really healthy—even #10 now.

# Mother Cows

In a typical cow-calf business such as the Bennetts', a herd of cows is bred each year and their calves are sold. But other factors, including a cow's age or a calf's lineage, help farmers decide which cows to sell and which calves to hold on to. The quality of a calf—and the price it brings at market — largely depends on its genes, half of which come from the cow, and half, from the bull. The Bennetts sire many of their calves by mail-ordering straws of semen from prize-winning champion bulls and impregnating their best cows through artificial insemination (AI).

**Dad:** The quality of the calf is what decides which cows we're going to AI and which we'll let the bull fertilize. It's interesting, but cows that raise great calves often look pretty poor themselves. While raising their calves, they're giving their all, so they end up looking scrawny or less fit. A cow that looks like a million dollars when she's nursing isn't necessarily the best mother, since she might not be producing the best calf. So we AI the ones that deliver the best-looking calves. It brings us a better sale.

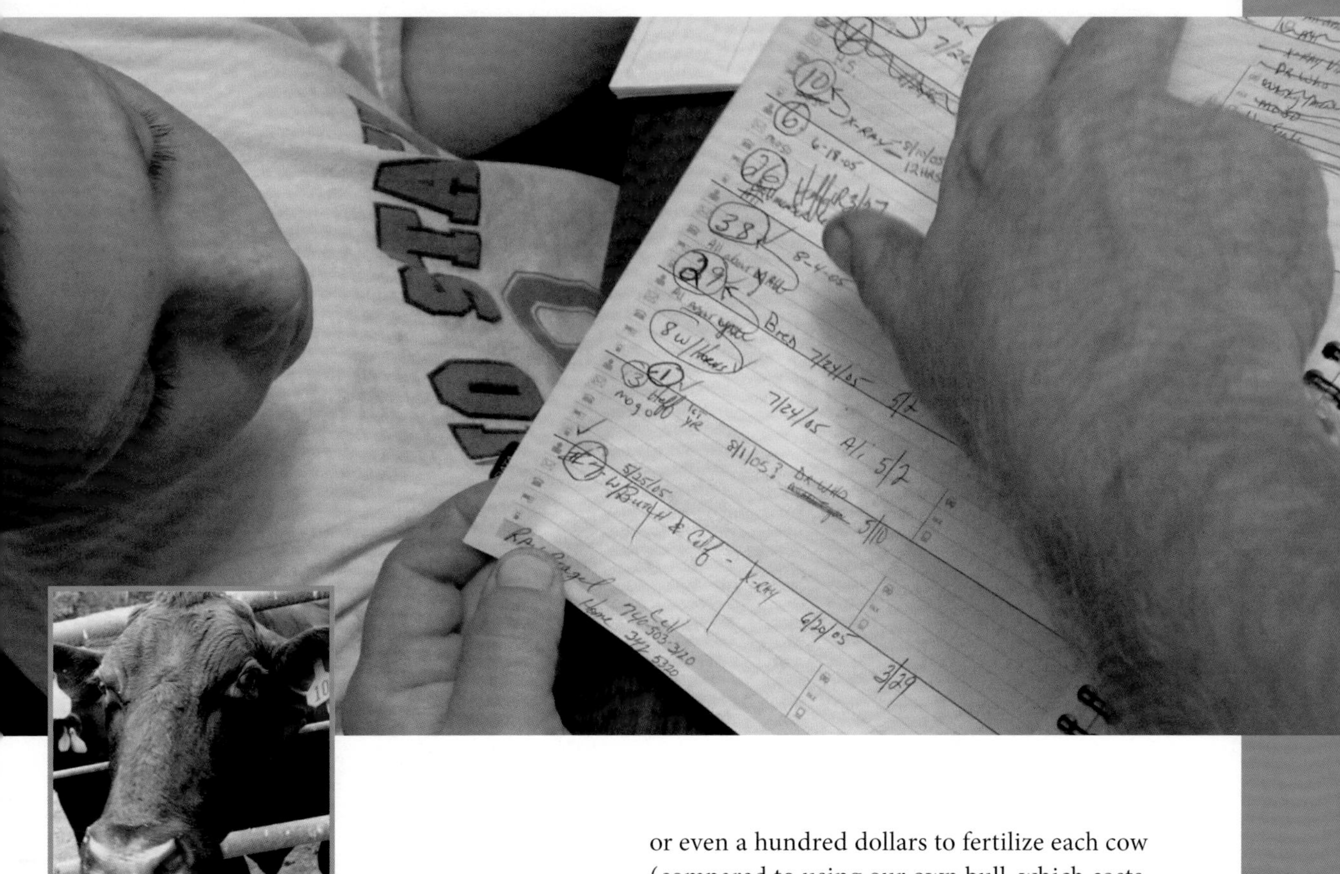

**Mom:** Number 10 is a special cow. Some cows will leave their calves with other mothers while they go and graze or whatever, but #10 won't let other cows babysit her calf, even for a little while. And the one year that she lost her calf, she tried to take on another cow's calf. She just wanted to nurse.

**Dad:** Maybe that's because she waited five years to have her own calf. She is one of our best mothers.

**Chase:** In the winter, we order straws of semen for our cows. It's more expensive—like twenty-five or even a hundred dollars to fertilize each cow (compared to using our own bull, which costs nothing)—but when you sell calves from champion bulls, you make that money back—and more.

We've ordered straws from the same bulls for a few years now. We've had calves from Mojo, Ali, Heatseeker, Doctor Who, X-Ray Vision, Totally Tuned—and some others I can't remember. Those better bulls also expand our herd's gene pool. (If our own bull fertilized every cow, all our calves would have his good and his bad qualities. And then, the next breeding season, he'd be fertilizing those cows again and any heifers—a cow who has yet to bear her first calf. But that's bad blood—bad animal husbandry.)

# Having Calves

**Grey:** You can tell a cow is close to having a baby when her belly gets really big and she lies down—or if a cow doesn't come up to eat when Dad puts in a round bale. (Usually, the cows come running when they hear the skid steer.) Chase walks the fields every day during birthing time, and he counts the big cows to see if any are missing. If one is, he goes looking to see if there are any new calves or any cows in labor.

**Cayne:** Angus's job is watching the cows, especially when they're going off to have calves by themselves. And he can find them. In the corral or the barn or the fields, he watches them like he is babysitting. Sometimes he does chase the cows, and sometimes the cows chase or kick at him. But mostly he's the boss of them.

**Chase:** Dad also knows when he gives the herd grain that if a cow is missing, it's either sick or having a calf. So I watch each calf and make sure it's okay, able to stand up. Dad writes it in the book when we have a calf. Then either Caleb or I try to separate the mother for a minute, putting her in the barn or behind a fence so Dad can tag the calf. He has a needle punch that goes right in the ear—like getting an ear pierced —and then Dad snaps the tag in the hole and gets out fast, or the mom might try to pummel him. Mothers don't like anyone near their babies.

The tags are different colors from different years and different companies, but one is the number tag and one is the fly-prevention tag that gets replaced each year in the same hole. When each calf is born, it gets ear-tagged immediately. That way, you can tell by looking at the cows which one's a male—that's a steer—and which one's a female—that's a cow.

**Mom:** Because "men are always right"—I can remember hearing this all the time—the male cows get tagged in the right ear! And the females have their left ear tagged.

**Cayne:** People think that it's just the males that have horns, but females can, too. It's just that certain breeds grow horns, and others—those are polled cows—don't grow horns.

**Dad:** We used to band the males at birth—that's a rubber band around their testicles that turns them into steers—but in the last couple of years, other farmers have wanted to buy bulls, so I stopped doing that so that when they buy our bulls, they have their reproductive organs.

# Losses

**Chase:** Round bales get old by mid-winter, and the cows want some fresh grass under the snow. But the field is just mud and snow. So the cows that calve first get moved out into a smaller field with their calves. That way, they don't get stuck in the mud the herd is going across back and forth and back on all day—and you can't collect the manure during the winter out there.

**Cayne:** A farm is a really muddy place, especially where the cows have been walking for a few days. When we had fifty cows, it was really a problem. Now we have half as many cows, so it's a lot better. Your boots get so heavy with mud when you're walking in the field, they sometimes stick, and if you keep walking, one will slip off!

**Grey:** We have something like twenty-seven or so calves every year, but we may lose one or two—four would be a *really* bad year. If we don't get a calf into the barn, it might hit the ground too hard and die. Or it can get too cold and die. Or it can get stuck in the mud and muck and suffocate.

**Mom:** That's why we changed things in the corral and feeding area and put in new drainage pipes and moved the cow/calf pairs to the other field where we can keep the young calves away from the mud.

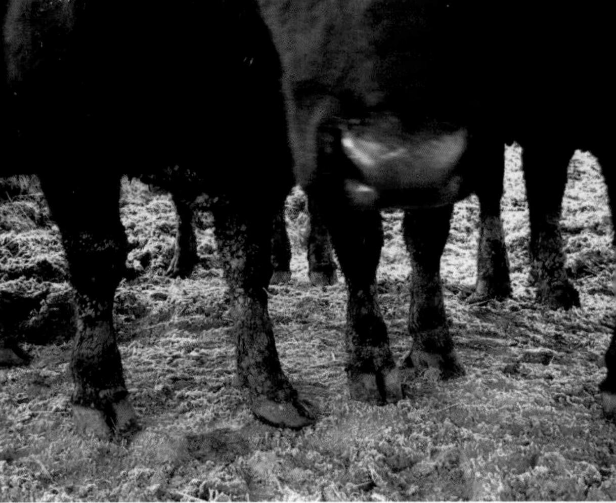

**Chase:** One February, a mother had a calf that wasn't doing well, and Dad carried it up into the barn. We used to have a pig hut there when we raised pigs. So we put straw in there and a tarp and a space heater, and the calf warmed up and made it through.

**Grey:** We had twins just once, but both died. Twins aren't as healthy as when just one calf grows in the mom's belly.

**Cayne:** If a cow dies, Dad scoops it up with the skid steer bucket and carries it over to the woods, far from the house, because it stinks for a while.

**Grey:** A few months later, there are just white bones left, because all the other creatures have cleaned it—and the flies and worms.

**Dad:** Yes, if a cow or calf dies a natural death, we take it to the woods where it can be a part of the cycle. Some creatures live by feeding on the death of other creatures. But if I have a cow that's died from something that could be contagious—or died for no reason I can tell—we bury that animal.

# The Bull, a Cow Named Darryl, and a Few Other Cows

**Cayne:** The bull was born right on our farm. He's four or five now. He has to be kept separate from the cows a lot of the time.

**Chase:** He's got the only job I'd want—he doesn't get sold for meat, he doesn't have calves nursing on him, he gets to graze pretty much all the time—and then he mates with all the cows that we're not AI-ing.

**Mom:** We got our first three cows in October of 1992. I remember the date because I was pregnant with Cayne, and we had nothing but a temporary fence to keep the cows in. So we were always having to chase cows that got out, and people would say, "How are you able to keep doing that, being pregnant and all?"

**Cayne:** One cow, #8, pushed my dad down this summer. Dad took along a bucket of grain to occupy #8 while he walked over to her new calf. (A cow will usually eat and ignore Dad while he makes sure the calf is healthy and tags it.) But #8's calf let out a bawl, and her mother charged Dad and knocked him over.

**Dad:** I got lucky. She got me right in the center of the chest with her head, and I fell right over. But I was able to kick at the cow with my boots and scramble under the fence before she could kick me or trample me. You don't want three-fourths of a ton of any cow standing on you.

**Chase:** Yes, we're selling #8 this year.

**Dad:** Now #1, she's the first cow we bought. We've had her fifteen years. She's one of the leaders of the herd, and she's responsible for the largest percentage of our cows. Her daughter was the first calf born on the farm, and we still have her, too.

**Chase:** We only have one named cow on the farm. That's Darryl, named after the person we got her from. You can tell her by the high point on her head and her sort of dumb expression. Now she is unique. She's actually nice. Tame. You can get close to her, and she likes you to pet her. Plus, she's always willing to help eat your food. If another cow is sick, you see, she'll help out and try to eat her food.

And Darryl's a good mother. She gives good milk, and her calves look really good, which means they bring more money at the auction. And the funniest thing is that her calves are just like her. They'll follow you in the field, and they'll want you to scratch their back and neck and behind the ears. They're all nice.

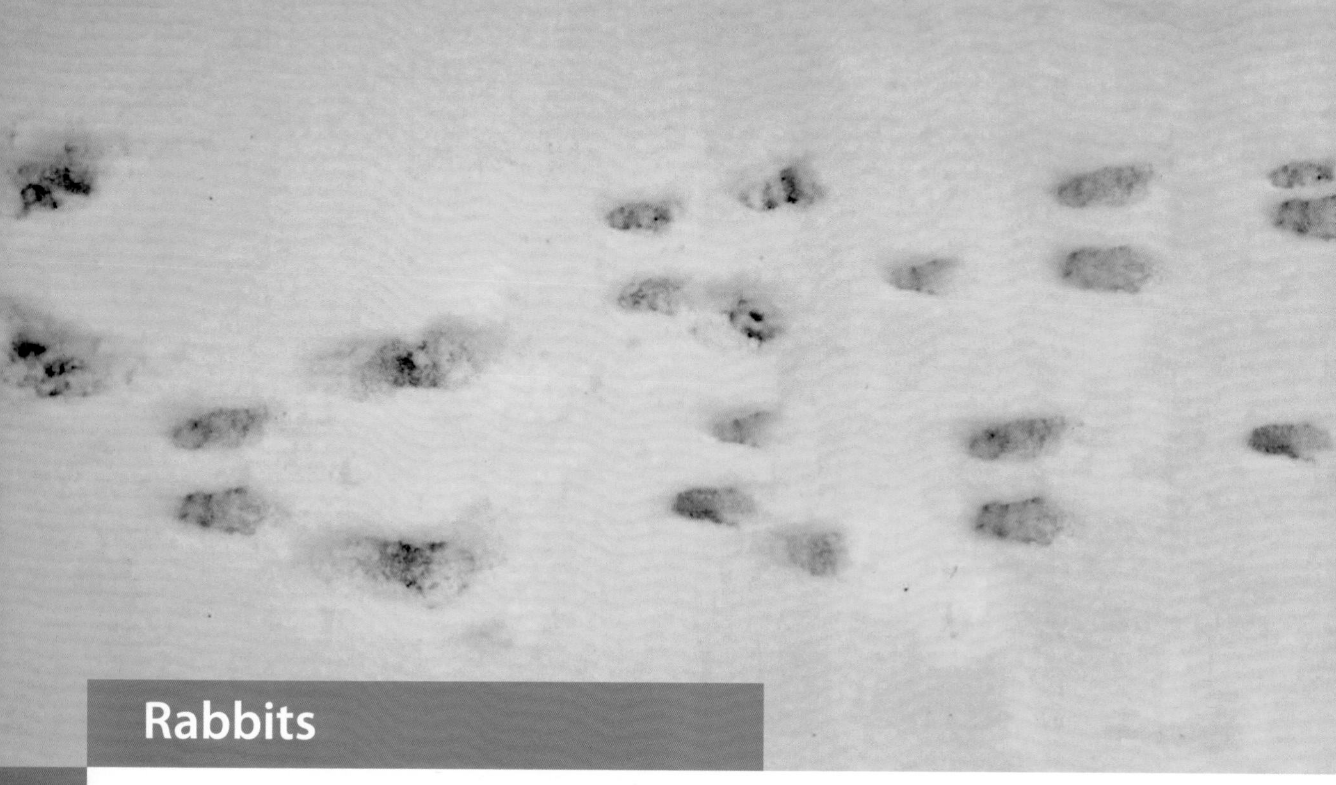

# Rabbits

Eastern cottontail rabbits are hunted by nearly every predator in the open country: house cats, owls, weasels, hawks, eagles, snakes, coyotes, dogs, and, of course, humans. They spend their days hiding in thick underbrush—blackberry and raspberry brambles, rose briars, tangled vines—and their nights grazing on nearby foods such as clover, berries, and tender plants.

Wintertime offers these creatures the least amount of protective cover and food (mostly the bark of nearby trees and brambles). It's no coincidence that their breeding season begins in February. Female rabbits, called does, typically give birth to four or five—and up to nine—offspring.

**Chase:** Rabbits can run up to fifteen miles an hour, and they can jump, in a single bound, at least ten feet—sometimes a lot more. I'm not sure how fast a beagle runs—let alone a three-legged beagle—but beagles are bred to be pack hunters, following a scent to chase and jump whatever's running ahead of them. And when dogs are hunting with us, they're supposed to drive the rabbit back toward the hunter, out in the open.

**Cayne:** Rabbit hunting is November through February. Basically, you just take out a small shotgun and kick the brush along the way. If you see a rabbit, you yell, "Here it goes!" Or if Bo flushes out a rabbit, we let the dog run it. The rabbit will usually run in a circle, and Bo gets to enjoy the run, too. It also makes a dog a better rabbit hunter if you let

the dog find rabbits this way. But sometimes the rabbits run straight into their holes, and we don't even get a shot.

**Dad:** Some people believe that a dog runs the rabbit in a circle right back to the hunter. But the truth is, the rabbit just runs in a circle, and the dog follows it. If a rabbit ran ten miles in a straight line, so would the dog.

**Mom:** I won't cook them unless the boys skin them first. Then I can make a rabbit stew—two or three rabbits will be a meal for everyone. And the kids eat pretty much everything I put on the table without thinking twice about it. They know whatever it is we're eating—chicken, cow, rabbit, turkey, fish—it's probably come from the farm.

# Spring

## by the Numbers

**27 calves**—number of births anticipated on the farm

**80 to 100 pounds**—average weight of a newborn calf

**9 months**—gestation period (from egg fertilization to giving birth) of a typical cow

**1 hour**—length of a typical labor and healthy delivery (A longer labor usually means trouble.)

**1 hour**—length of time it takes before a newborn calf stands and walks

**6 to 8 gallons**—amount of milk a nursing cow produces every day

**2 gallons**—amount of water needed for a cow to produce one gallon of milk

**15 to 35 gallons**—amount of water a beef cow will need in one day

**3 to 5 pounds**—average weight of a hen bred for egg laying

**6 months**—average age when a hen on the Bennett farm lays its first egg

**259 eggs**—average number that a hen will produce in a year

**550 gallons**—amount of farm diesel fuel consumed by the Bennett machines in one year

**26 feet**—the new pond's deepest part

**1,200 fingerlings**—number of newly hatched fish delivered to the pond

# Trees

When European settlers arrived in Ohio more than two hundred years ago, forests covered 95 percent of the land. Within a hundred years, only 10 percent of the forests remained. Trees were cleared to create housing developments, grazing land, fields of corn or soybean, and, in the Bennetts' area, strip mines and quarries. A great replanting effort occurred during the 1930s and then again in 1965, in a targeted effort to reclaim barren areas surrounding strip mines.

Today 31 percent of the state is forested. Of that, 87 percent is owned by families such as the Bennetts. According to the Ohio Division of Forestry, the state grows one billion board feet of wood in a year, an amount that is almost three times greater than the wood harvested in a year.

Board feet is the standard unit of measure for timber (timber being trees prepared to be made into lumber). Picture a one-inch-thick square of wood that's twelve inches on all four sides: That's one board foot, or 144 cubic inches.

**Dad:** The oldest trees on the property are black cherries, black walnuts, and sugar maples (also called hard maples). Before we timbered the woods, these trees were maybe eighty or ninety years old. The beams in our house are timbers from the original farm building built in 1844—twenty years before the Civil War. That means the timbers were probably 120 years old when they were cut, so they were growing before the War of Independence! Think of how many storms, blizzards, and winds this house has endured.

**Mom:** I think of all the meals that were cooked in this house, all the children who were born or lived here, all the people who stood where we're standing.

**Caleb:** Old houses are full of surprises—things you never see now—like walls made of horsehair plaster. I don't know how that's constructed, but when I've torn out a wall as we've redone a room, there's this thick plaster with fibers in it, all slathered on top of wood strips. Now our new walls are made of drywall skimmed with plaster.

**Chase:** There are houses not even one mile from here that are just being built. Everything in those places is brand new—not like here. We're living at a farm that Dad knew when he was growing up. It was the grandparents' home of people he knew. And probably his grandparents knew—you know, "that farm on the bend of Hopewell Indian Road" — that's now our place.

**Dad:** We had one sixty-foot timber in the barn. It was hand-hewn. Just imagine the height of that tree when it was cut. To get a timber that's fifteen inches by fifteen inches and sixty feet long, the tree had to have towered over this land. Even the skinny end had to have a fifteen-inch diameter.

To build onto our house, we waited twelve years and had the land timbered. Those mature trees provided us with the money. A single black cherry that's straight and large—no limbs, no knots, just shooting straight up—can bring three thousand dollars for making veneer. But hard maples provided most of the timber, which probably brought three hundred to five hundred dollars per tree.

# A Tree House, a Fort, an Orchard, and a Garden

**Grey:** This new one is practically mine, and it's not finished. Cayne told me about building a tree house at his friend's, so Mom and I pounded in the boards and then the landing on the giant tree beside the house. And then everyone wanted to come up.

**Caleb:** When I was about Grey's age, I made a fort, too, with a window, a tin roof, and doors—it was a pig pen originally, but we moved it to the back of the property. It was a cool place to hang out. It was near the old orchard. The apple trees there didn't produce more than tiny apples—bumpy, spotted ones—but Dad remembers hearing that Johnny Appleseed went right through this area and that all our trees are descended from those he planted around here.

**Chase:** The cows like those apples. They'll graze on the fallen ones, and we like to hand-feed them to the cows, too.

**Ali:** But Mom and I planted apple, peach, and nectarine trees so we could have our own fruit. All the trees came in a long box! We dug holes when the ground was not frozen and stood each tree down in the hole. Then they weren't much taller than me! I know we won't pick anything for a couple of years. But maybe when I'm ten, we'll have fruit. We might plant a garden, too, this summer, and then I'll be able to pick things even this year!

**Mom:** We used to garden every year, but juggling babies and young kids along with the house and farm, well, a garden's not possible every year. So what we used to grow—corn, peppers, cucumbers, tomatoes—we get from neighbors and friends.

**Caleb:** Yeah, I used to go outside in the summer with a salt shaker, and Brandon and I would pick tomatoes from the garden, pulling out our t-shirts to make a hammock so that we could carry a load of them out to our fort where we'd eat the tomatoes with salt—and that was lunch.

# Fences

**Miles of uninterrupted fence make it possible for the Bennetts to keep their cows safe and on their property. The fences are made of wires stretched between wooden posts. Each span contains five wires, two of which carry a mild electric charge. It's the shock—as well as the surprise of it—that trains the cows to keep back.**

**Chase:** We have a springtime field, our smallest, for calves—and that's fenced. Then we have the big field where we feed the herd with round bales—and that's fenced. During the summer, cows graze in the winter field, the middle field, and out on two big fields in the back—and they're all fenced. There's one more field at the top of the property that we use for making hay, but during the fall, the cows graze there, too, on the good grass. And it's fenced, too, like all the others, with five wires on each span between the posts. Some people wonder why we don't have wooden fences, but that would be expensive and not as good at keeping in cows.

**Cayne:** We're always repairing the fences, too, because trees fall on them, and bushes and vines tangle on the wires. We have to get the trees off and replace wire or posts that are rotten.

**Caleb:** The hardest part isn't making the wires tight and straight; a ratchet will cinch them up tight. But to get the steeples to go in straight and stay in —that's a skill. (And they're not staples—they're steeples. They're like a nail with two sharp points bent into a skinny U.)

**Dad:** Either the steeples come out, and that's a problem, or the vines and the brush will become the ground for the electricity, and that shorts out the line, so then the fence isn't effective.

**Chase:** When we first put in a fence, we use a post pounder. It's like a huge, heavy hammer that knocks the poles into the ground. Each pole is actually eight feet tall, but about four feet is buried.

**Grey:** When we have a fence turned off—like if we're working on it or needing to climb over and back a lot—then the cows figure out the coast is clear, and they stick their heads through because the hay bales that they aren't supposed to eat yet are just on the other side. Or they try to eat the grass around the pond. So when Dad switches the current back on, you can see them all jerk back to their side of the fence.

**Chase:** Oh, I've been shocked plenty. It's a real jolt, and your arm feels numb for a few seconds. The closer you are to the charger, the stronger the shock. And you better not be standing in water or be walking barefoot, because then the current would really hurt. And I remember Dad saying that if you are holding on to the fence and then you hold someone else, you don't get shocked—the person you're holding gets the zap.

# Human Power and Horsepower (But No Horses)

The Bennett family shares the farm work—and profits—with the Davy family, who live three miles away. Bill Davy and his son Josh join in the ongoing seasonal tasks, and younger son Dylan helps with the larger projects. The two fathers and the two older boys contribute most of the muscle power as well as the know-how for keeping the machines in working order: even a smaller farm requires a fleet of machinery—they're like another herd of creatures that require care and tending.

"And they all run on diesel," Dad explains. "Now farm diesel is different from the diesel that goes into cars. It comes with a red tint. Otherwise, it's the same fuel. But because farmers don't pay tax on their farm fuel, it's illegal to be on the road with a car that's using farm diesel."

Here are Chase and Caleb's brief descriptions of some of the machines on their farm:

**Skid Steer** It has tracks that surround the wheels like on a bulldozer. To maneuver, you push either one or both steering bars. That allows the machine to plant one wheel in place so the other side can pivot around it. We attach the bale spear or the slurry bucket (for wet manure and for lifting us up to pick grapes). Basically it's a front-end loader on a small bulldozer that we use for moving dirt, mud, and manure.

**Three Big Tractors** We have all Ford 7000s. They're high-crop, which means they sit up higher than other tractors. One has a front-end loader on it, which we use for moving hay, and the other two are working tractors for towing, baling, tedding, and mowing.

**Hay Bine/Sickle-Bar Mower** Like a hair clipper, this machine has one stationary set of teeth and one moving set of teeth. The grass catches between them and is trimmed off. And the hay bine has two rubber wheels that are grooved, which crimp and press the hay before it hits the ground. They crack each strand, which helps the hay dry more quickly. This machine hooks up to the tractor, connected by a power take-off shaft—or PTO—which powers every piece of equipment we pull.

**Disk Bine** It's another kind of mower with disks that spin to cut the grass. And it has to be timed every year so the spinners are aligned. Each unit covers one foot of grass with its blades—a twelve-foot disk bine has twelve mowing units.

**Farm Cart** Some people use this vehicle as a golf cart, but out here, it's a farm cart. Cayne and Grey have a driver's license for that cart.

**Riding Lawnmower** The 18-horsepower diesel mower turns nine hours of mowing into three hours. Since we have to mow about five acres, this is a real necessity.

**Hay Rake** The tractor pulls the rake, which isn't motorized. It has angled fingers that form circular rakes that barely touch the ground. The rakes twirl and pull all the cut hay into a narrower swath called a windrow, which is just a longer, thinner pile that the wind can dry more quickly.

**Dad:** One time, Josh and Caleb were loading the spreader—and they had loaded it well past full—and I said, "You realize that when you fill it that full, if the chains break, there's only one way to get the manure out of there to repair it." So they went out to the field, and half a load later, they were right back in the barn, shoveling out the manure by hand so they could get in there and repair the chains. I couldn't help but laugh, since it's not often that a parent just happens to be proven right immediately after offering the advice.

**Manure Spreader** This is a special trailer we drag behind a tractor. You fill the front part with manure, and it has several flippers that spin around, pushing manure to the back of the spreader, where blades fling bits in a wide swath across the field. Whenever we clean the barn, we load and run the spreader about twenty-five times to cover the fields.

**Bale Spear** This is a hook that attaches to the front of the tractor or the skid steer. You can put one spear on the back or one on the front so you can stab a round bale and then carry it wherever you need to go.

**Bush Hog** This is our utility mower: a low, flat square that's hauled by the tractor. It's heavy-duty enough to chop small trees, bushes, and the thorny multi-flora roses that grow wild. It has two blades that spin inside—but they really tear up the grass, so you don't want to use that for the hay you're baling.

Multi-flora roses are non-native, tenacious, fast-growing roses first offered to farmers by the U.S. Soil Conservation Service in the 1930s as "a living fence" for erosion control or confining livestock. Ohio and several other states now classify the plant as a "noxious weed" because it's so invasive that it upsets local ecosystems.

**Gravity Wagon** We hook this on a tractor and drive over to Ted's house to get our feed corn. He has a huge harvester with a grain chute that fills the wagon. Once it's home, it just sits in the barn near the cows, and all you do is pull a lever, and gravity funnels the corn down and into a feed bucket.

**Round-Baler** Towed behind a tractor, the round baler has belts inside that roll the mown hay into a bale with a diameter of four to six feet. It wraps each rolled bale in mesh and then releases it.

**Hay Elevator** This revolutionized our way of handling the square bales. Now we don't have to throw every bale from the wagon up six or seven feet to the loft—which was a ton of work. The elevator lets you heave a bale from the wagon onto the bottom of the track, and its claws convey the bale up the plank to the loft, where it falls off. Then someone else carries the bale wherever the bales are being stacked.

**Hay Wagons** These are flat, wooden trailers we use for hauling square bales. Our favorite is one that Dad got at an auction. It's got a cage, and so when the baler kicks a square bale into the air, it can land back there wherever, and you don't have to catch each one. That wagon can be loaded with just the person who's driving the tractor.

**Ali:** My tractor doesn't do anything. You hit a button and nothing happens. But you can pedal, and it can move. I'll have to be way bigger to drive one of Dad's tractors—but I don't really want to anyway.

## Chase's Radish Experiment

**Chase:** All you hear about out here is fertilizer. And everywhere you see ads for Miracle Gro and how that's the big thing to make everything grow bigger. And there are other brands, too, that are like two dollars less for a package. And our family tries to be economical. So maybe for two months, for seventh grade science fair, I did a test.

I had a control group of radish seedlings that only got water. Another group got the expensive stuff. A third group got the less expensive growing stuff. After two or three weeks, the seedlings with the off-brand food were ahead by one or two inches. I built a tri-board, took pictures of all the plants, and made a chart to show my hypothesis and how I tested it. I got a superior, and then a superior at the district science fair. But the funny thing is, we don't really use fertilizer here, since we have manure sort of built in.

# Driving with Angus

**Grey:** Just for fun, we drive the old farm cart around our fields, but it's also for getting work done—like we take all the tools we need when we're rebuilding fences. Or if Dad forgets something at the house, we can drive up and get whatever it is.

**Caleb:** But wherever we go, Angus runs ten yards in front of us. I don't know how he can just run and run like that. Tires me out just watching him.

**Grey:** He always races ahead of the cart, the different tractors, whatever the tractor is pulling, the bobcat, the bush hog—everything but the regular cars. He just knows better, and he never leaves the farm or goes onto the road. But the farm equipment? He runs in front, and then looks sideways, looks backwards at you, and then he runs ahead, and then stops and looks, and switches back every few seconds to see where you are and how fast you are moving. He just likes to be in front. In his brain, I think, Angus figures he is herding everything. He thinks he is making you go.

Or else Angus just runs over to you and pushes his head between your arm and your body so you can pet him.

**Cayne:** Dad made up fake driver's licenses for all of us, and if we do something bad on the cart, we have to be off it for three or four days. Or if we aren't carrying our license with us, we have to be off it for a week. Some rules: You're not allowed to chase people when you're driving. You can't floor it when you're taking someone somewhere and there's a sharp turn—that kind of thing.

**Grey:** The cart only goes five or ten miles per hour, I think, but that's faster than running even. Ali can't drive it yet because she can't see over the wheel and also push the pedal. I still have to lean to see around the steering wheel. But it's really safe since there's no other traffic besides cows, and they're not moving a lot.

**Cayne:** Some people out here have four-wheelers, which go a lot faster than the farm cart. Those are more like a motorcycle with four wheels, where your thumb on the handle-lever increases your speed. And you get good mileage on those. We have about 150 acres. You can't drive everywhere in the woods, but I have walked in almost all the woods. Not all at once, since that would take... I don't know how long!

# Corralling the Cows

**Chase:** Once a year, in the spring, we get all the cows into the big corral, and then we move them into a smaller part that's separated by gates. Next we kind of run the cows toward the head gate so they're in single file. Then we can move each cow forward, one at a time.

**Dad:** When all the cows go through the chute into the head gate, we can worm them and give them new fly tags, which contain a solution that goes on the ear and spreads across their bodies —it even spreads to their calves since they're always brushing up against their mothers. And every other year, we vaccinate, too, for whatever diseases the vet recommends.

**Chase:** It's best to have at least three people: One person stands at the head gate, ready to shut it as soon as the cow comes forward; one person goes behind and drops a bar behind the cow's knees so it can't back out; and one person works to move them through the chute.

Usually, that's Bill, since it can be dangerous—cows can kick you or kick the gate. Some people don't know this, but cows prefer to kick to the side; you're usually safe so long as you're straight behind them.

If nothing else, those forty-eight cows produced 576 tons of manure in a year (that's 1,152,000 pounds), much of which the Bennetts had to remove, pile up to dry, and spread over the pastures.

Our friend Rod welded these movable metal gates, so now we can adjust the corrals to make more room, to confine just one or two cows, to cut out a place just for the calves, or to help when it comes time to separate the herd for sale.

**Cayne:** Farm work is not like it used to be. When I was really, really little, we always did stuff with the cows every day. Working in the corral. Out in the field. I think we had maybe forty-eight cows at one point. So that's some of the reason. But things are a lot more organized now.

# Manure

**Chase:** Every month, we clean the barn stalls, haul the manure outside to dry, and then sometimes put down stone, or grindings—that's just ground-up roads—which works really well to keep the floor of the stalls drier. And this year we're putting in a new drainage system. This is just to keep the ground firmer, since the cows pee and poop and walk back and forth over the same ground all the time.

**Grey:** The amount of manure depends on how many cows and how big the cows are. In a week, older cows can make enough manure to be standing up to their ankles in it. And in three weeks, we have to get the whole barn shoveled out.

So, first we use the skid steer. After that, we get out the pitchforks and shovels and make a huge pile of the manure. Then Dad or Caleb drives the Bobcat's bucket into the piles and carries it over to the manure pile. And it has to dry there outside the barn.

It takes a while to dry sometimes. Then Dad usually gets the skid steer, loads as much as he can in the bucket, and then it carries the manure to the spreader and dumps it in. After a few loads, Caleb drives out into the field. The spreader has chains that move manure to propellers at the end of the spreader, and those spinning blades fling chunks of the manure pretty evenly all over the field.

**Caleb:** I usually fertilize the main fields, like right outside around the house and behind the barn and the large field where the old barn used to be. We spread maybe three times during the summer.

**Grey:** Manure spreading is kind of like our version of the oxygen-and-carbon-dioxide cycle with plants. Cows have a deal with hay. We clean the barn a few times a year and move their manure out to dry in a pile. Then we spread it on a field, and that makes the hay grow faster, bigger, better. And then the cows eat that. So it's a cycle.

## Smell? What Smell?

**Grey:** The biggest manure pile ever was ten feet high. We play who can get to the top fastest or king of the mountain and shove each other off. Mom says we are happiest when we are dirty, and that it's really gross to play on a mountain of cow crap.

**Chase:** Sometimes people will come over and say, "What's that smell?" and we don't know what they're talking about. When it's dry, manure hardly smells.

**Grey:** Yeah, what smell? I don't even smell anything. I was born here, and every day there's been the manure smell—and it's still here. It's just the scent of fresh air from what I know.

**Cayne:** You do always get dirty here. We don't care if manure gets on us—we just shower. We have outside clothes, and if we get dirty and wet, we have to take them off when we come in. But if we want to go out again, we have to wear the same things again since Mom doesn't want to do laundry all day.

**Chase:** Josh, especially, always finds a way to get muddy and manure-y. It seems like he tries to. Like once he was in a tractor and jumped down into the mud, but it was really pretty soft manure, and both feet got stuck deep. He teetered and just fell over, back first, and made a whole body print in the mud. Josh is our comic relief.

# Making Hay

Growing feed for the cattle is the Bennetts' primary agricultural effort. Three times during the growing season, they harvest—mow, rake, bale, and store—the fields' mix of alfalfa and orchard grass. Freshly cut grass is a smell the cows, and the kids, love. While the adults work the actual mowers and balers, all four Bennett boys—and, usually, the two Davy boys—help with the making of square bales, offloading the bales and sending them up the conveyor to the loft, where they are stacked for the seasons ahead. The loft is also where all the cats live—and no small number of mice.

**Chase:** Making hay is a big part of cow farming. And if you don't bale your own, you'll be at the mercy of the seller. That's expensive, buying it all.

Baling hay is sort of complicated, but there are four steps, really. First we use the disk mower—it has disks that slice the grass pretty neatly so that it lands in rows about six feet wide.

**Caleb:** Either Dad, Josh, Bill, or I mow. It takes quite a while because you can't go very fast and our fields are pretty large. (Maybe not compared to ranches out west, but still huge.) If it looks like rain, we don't mow, because that can cause the hay to rot or take too long to dry. Wind and warmer temperatures, on the other hand, really help to dry the hay.

**Chase:** Tedding is next. Basically the tractor pulls the tedder, which has two spinning metal wheels with forks along the bottom that pick up the hay and toss it, spreading it out so that it dries faster and better.

**Caleb:** It not only spreads the hay, but also flips it as it picks it up, so that the underside can dry. We do the tedding about a day after mowing, depending on weather.

**Chase:** Then the rake machine picks up two rows of the cut grass and makes one thicker, narrower row. It has three pairs of round rakes that spin as the tractor pulls the rake over the hay. The spinners squeeze the cuttings closer into one narrow row about three feet wide and one foot tall. (The size depends on how high the hay was before moving.) Then we have two different machines for baling—but in the spring, it's mostly round bales.

The old saying, "you have to make hay while the sun shines," has two meanings for the Bennetts. One is that farmers want the sun's warmth to dry the hay before baling it. "The other is that, in ideal conditions, with the plentiful spring- or early-summer grass, you've got to make all the bales you can," Dad says. "There's no making hay in the dead of winter if you run low."

**Ali:** Only the skid steer can move those bales, but if one of the boys helps me, I can climb up a bale—or I can climb up by myself if there are two bales close together.

**Chase:** For round bales, we use the round-bale machine, which also has these arms that circle and spin the hay inside, compacting it into a tight, heavy roll. Then the machine backs up, and you pull a cord that winds around the bale. The chute opens, and the hay bale rolls out. It's pretty amazing.

**Dad:** The tractor pulls the baler. Then we use the bale spears or the wagons and haul the finished bales off the field—you don't want a hundred dead spots on the field —and stack them near the barn.

# Chickens

**Dad:** At about fifty days, meat chickens are ready to be butchered. They're called broilers or fryers, because their meat is young and tender, and they don't need to be stewed or cooked a long time to get them tender. (Stewing chickens are older and tougher.) We picked one day to butcher the meat chickens, all six. I slit their throats with a knife, and then the kids helped pluck off the feathers. That does take some time. If you dip the whole chicken in hot water for half a minute, the feathers are easier to remove. Then I cleaned the birds, took out the entrails, scrubbed the meat in the sink, and brought them inside so Mom could cook them.

**Mom:** One of these larger chickens is a good meal for all of us. But we don't have the room or the time to raise as many chickens as our family eats in a year. Plus, butchering was truly a hassle—a good experience for the kids raising the chickens, but too much time for an every-week meal.

**Grey:** From the new egg-laying chickens, we will get one or two or three or four eggs each day from the whole coop. Every day we check for eggs. A hen will run away, so you can just reach right in and take the egg, but if there's a rooster nearby, he will stand his ground. An old chicken will sometimes chase you, and roosters will even try to peck you with their beaks—and that can make you bleed. Sometimes when you are walking away—if you turn your back—they charge you, and that scares you.

"Want my favorite recipe for an old rooster?" Dad offers. "Place it in a slow cooker on low for, oh, about a week, and then serve it with some mashed potatoes —and you'll have mashed potatoes and a rooster that's still tough as a shoe."

Especially Ali. The two old chickens still chase Ali because she is small, so she likes to scream when they get near her.

But if a hen is already sitting on her egg, she'll sometimes fluff up like she's really big. Then either Cayne or I will take a stick and nudge her out of the way, and the other person grabs the egg.

**Mom:** A dozen eggs aren't quite enough for our breakfast. Every Saturday at least, we have eggs. And we're always having people over or giving eggs to relatives. It's not that we are saving so much money, but fresh eggs are a world of difference from store-bought eggs that are probably weeks—or maybe months—old. The yolks are yellower, plumper, and rounder, and the egg's flavor is just better.

# Cow on the Loose?

**Cayne:** At the front of our driveway, our property has another strip that's a neighbor's, and his cows get out a lot. He doesn't have an electric fence along our driveway, so when a cow gets out, we have to call him.

The one weekend that Grey and I put out our new minnow trap in the little stream that runs between the two properties, one of our neighbor's calves got loose. It just wedged through an opening in the broken fence. We didn't know that. And when we went to check the minnow trap, it was crunched in the middle. The new trap! And we couldn't figure out what happened—we had just put it in the water that morning. Then we figured out it was a cow's hoof that crushed it.

**Grey:** Rounding up a loose cow is sometimes hard. It's not like we get up on horses with a lasso or any of that.

**Dad:** Older cows will follow a bucket and a little grain. So if they get out, they know where they're allowed to be and where they're supposed to be, and they're usually easy to move. The boys can make a wall of people and angle the cow in the direction we need it to go. But calves? Calves are like kids—they don't know where they're supposed to be or what they're supposed to be doing. Then, it's best to drive the mothers where you want the calves to follow.

# More Calves

Some cows in the herd continue to give birth well into spring, even as the first cows that already gave birth approach the time to be fertilized again, either by artificial insemination (AI) or by the resident bull. Although each season brings routine changes for the herd and specific responsibilities for the family members, each animal's reproductive cycle is slightly different.

**Chase:** We like to wait a few months after delivery for the mother cow to be AI-ed again for the next year's calf. A cow's heat cycle is about twenty-one days, and then they're pregnant for about nine months—just like humans—before they give birth.

**Caleb:** Gomer is a tan Jersey bull with white around his nose. He wants to mate with the cows that are in heat, but at the vet school at Ohio State, they fixed him so his sperm doesn't come out. Most gomers are Jerseys, because they're lighter than Angus cows, so they're not too strong or too heavy for a new mother.

**Cayne:** When Gomer jumps on a cow, we know that she's in heat and ready to get pregnant. But he can't make her pregnant. He only lets us know when we should call Ray and have him come over and AI the cow.

**Chase:** Calves are really fragile when they're born. Normally, a cow will give birth standing up. (In a troubled birth, the cow will lie down on her side.)

The calf falls down—and it's a long fall—so they can injure their legs because they're so weak and haven't ever stood before. A calf starts breathing when it hits the ground. Sometimes it's still surrounded by the birth sac—or its head is just sticking out of it. So the mother turns quickly and cleans the calf.

**Cayne:** One way you know a cow is ready to have a calf is that she will hide or go into the woods, and we will have to find her. Sometimes one will be down near the stream, almost camouflaged by the weeds and vines. But our dog Angus is great at that. You can also tell a cow is ready to deliver because her milk bag swells up so she can feed the baby.

**Dad:** Here's how you know a calf's in trouble: If you see two hooves coming out of the mother, and they're bending down, that's good—that means those are the front hooves. But if the two hooves are bending up toward the sky that means those are the rear hooves—a breech birth—and that's hard.

**Cayne:** If a calf is coming out backwards, Dad usually needs to hook a chain to the calf's feet to help pull out the baby.

**Chase:** That's why it's safer if the calves are born in or near the barn. New mothers sometimes have calves that are turned around, or they don't know what to do after the calf is born. If the cow is somewhere else, and you do need to pull the calf out, you have to take all the equipment—a calf puller and chains and a pulley device called a come-along.

**Cayne:** When we find a newborn calf, we tag it (Dad does) so we know which baby goes with which mom. Dad writes it on his calendar. The mom doesn't like us near her calf, which is probably why she hides. She doesn't want us to find it and bother her. And it makes her mad when Dad tags them. Once a cow tackled Dad and bucked him with her head to make him get away from the calf.

**Dad:** Calves are with their mothers for six months—max. After a cow gives birth, she breeds two to three months later. So she's nursing a calf and raising a calf in her belly for three months, and so that's like supporting three bodies. So that means it's time to sell. The calves get weaned off milk and onto hay and grain in the barn.

**Chase:** You can't just leave them in the pasture, because they have such a strong bond that no fence in the county could keep a calf from her mother and a mother from her calf. So we have to confine the calves to the barn.

**Dad:** That lasts about five days, and their bawling is really annoying. There's a farmer saying that goes, "If you wean on a full moon, that will cut the bawling time in half." We usually try to put the calves and cows two fields apart. If they can't hear one another bawling, they don't call back and forth. Then they have no choice. They have to go on without each other.

# Exploring the Land

**Caleb:** Our acres are pretty diverse, and that means a lot of habitats for various animals. Aside from the pastures, we have wooded areas, a stream, smaller creeks, hills and valleys, and then other fields surround us, so that's mostly what we see of our neighbors.

The bridge across our creek sometimes washes out. Trees fall across the drive. There are other times that the driveway is like a small creek, and there are deep holes that you have to fill with stones to get the cars across. Most of that falls to me to do.

**Grey:** In the creek or on the driveway or in the woods—we're always seeing interesting things you'd hardly ever see in a city. At least alive. Like we have snapping turtles, box turtles, painted turtles. Tree frogs and bullfrogs.

**For all hard-shell turtles such as painted-, box-, and snapping turtles, temperature determines the sex of each emerging hatchling. A warmer egg near the top of a nest will hatch out a female. A cooler egg toward the bottom of a nest will hatch out a male.**

**Cayne:** We find salamanders and crawdads in the streams—and minnows, of course. Snakes—mostly garter snakes, black snakes—nothing poisonous, I don't think. I don't really like snakes. No one in the family does.

**Chase:** We see coyotes, more now than we used to. They're usually quiet and you don't hear them, but sometimes at night you can hear them talking to one another. I guess there are foxes here, too. I haven't seen them. Of course, my Uncle Cliff traps all kinds of animals: possums, raccoons, muskrats, beaver, skunk, mink.

**Cayne:** One place we always find nests is in the pinecone trees beside the barn. The birds use pine needles and cows' hairs in their nests. They probably find the hairs where the cows rubbed against the tree bark or in the barn where they like to rub.

**Grey:** We see lots of hawks and turkey vultures. We hear owls, but they're usually only out at night, and we don't see them. There's a bald eagle nest, too, not very far from here.

**Caleb:** We have one pond where we find snapping turtles, which are good eating, even though they're incredibly hard to clean. (Plus, like most reptiles, they keep moving even after they're dead.) But once you skin them, you can chop the meat and make this soup that's delicious.

My grandmother used to tell me that if you take a turtle far from its home and let it go—no matter how far away—it will find its way back to the body of water where it was born. I don't know if that's true, but it sounds good.

**Caleb's grandmother is right . . . up to a certain point—or distance, to be specific. Turtles do have a natural instinct to return to their original birth site to breed. Research on sea turtles, in particular, suggests that they navigate using the Earth's magnetic fields and their own internal magnetic compass. (Whales, trout, honeybees, and pigeons also orient their journeys this way.) But biologists have also shown that moving a box turtle more than half a mile from its territory will disrupt its breeding cycle as it aimlessly searches for that familiar place.**

But Josh and I have caught a few snappers. "Old-timers" say that a turtle offers seven different flavors in its meat. They catch snappers the way they catch catfish, by "noodling," which means the "noodler" wades along the shores of a stream, poking his arm into muskrat holes and among the big roots of shoreline trees, hoping to grab a snapper by the tail and pull it out. I'd prefer to keep all ten of my fingers and use a hook with some rotten meat for catching snappers.

**Chase:** And let me tell you, the bait that Josh stuck on the hooks—he says the more rotten the meat, the more the turtles will pick up on the stink—that was worse than anything I've smelled. And I live on a farm where we have a fair amount of stink.

# Grapevines

**More than fifty species of wild grapes grow in the Midwest, including such varieties as riverbank grapes, frost grapes, fox grapes, summer grapes, pigeon grapes, and possum grapes. They bear considerably smaller fruit than grapes grown for the table, such as the Concord grapes that the Bennett family planted. While these climbing shrubs do provide important food for birds, deer, and other wildlife, old grapevines can climb a tree's trunk and produce such a thick canopy of large leaves that they will hoard all the sunlight and kill the tree.**

**Grey:** The thing about grapevines is that if you pull down hard on one, if it slips even a little, you shouldn't swing on it. Vines need to be about as round as your wrist, and they have to be strong and bendable. We have a lot of vines, and we go out and swing on them, but we usually end up breaking half of those we find. I was really high once, and the vine broke free—and I landed right on my back. It hurt, but I was okay.

**Cayne:** When the older boys shove us, we swing a lot higher and farther. Like six feet off the ground, or maybe twelve feet!

**Ali:** I like how you can feel the wind blowing through your hair when you're swinging.

**Chase:** We have one huge vine that went along the cow fence and then along the creek. You could swing from the hill out over the creek and then—if you held on—swing right back to the top of the hill.

**Grey:** If you find a skinny vine that you can break with your hand, you can get water from it! It's not grape juice—it's just water, but really sweet—and it will drip right into your mouth.

**Cayne:** Plain, pure water, so in case you're really thirsty out in the woods, there's grapevine water!

# The New Pond

**Farmers often create a pond on their property to help with water conservation, to irrigate crops or feed livestock, to supply water in case of a fire, or simply to provide a nearby spot for fishing, skating, and swimming.**

**Caleb:** Our farm always had this one spring that ran down the hillside, so when we finally had our own pond dug, the trucks started at the spring and then dug a really deep pit to catch the water. Then they built up the sides to form the dam. The whole pond is just under an acre. It was just another part of the pasture—kind of a gully where the cows always liked to drink. The cows also have the creek for water. During the summer, that's about the only place you'll find them, standing there in the shade.

**Chase:** It took the digging crew six months, finishing about October. Then it took rain, snow, and the spring water to fill the pond—by about April.

**Dad:** The guys brought in track hoes, bulldozers, and a sheep's foot, which is what packs down the dam. (It's like a heavy rolling pin with lots of flat prongs on it, so a huge amount of weight bears down on just a few points.) They drove it over and over and over the dam, packing down each bit so no water could leak through.

**Cayne:** When we were building the pond, there were huge hills of dirt for weeks and weeks. The pond had to be deep, so tons of dirt and clay piled up to make the tall sides. The bottom, down low there, had small walls of dirt separating different parts of it while it was being dug. Some water was only about a foot deep, and the sun's heat made it very warm there. We called that our hot tub, and we would sit in the water, even though the clay made it muddy brown.

**Grey:** Then a different guy came in a truck that had a tank full of water and fish, like grass carp, walleye, and sunfish. There were lots of different kinds and colors, and they were all about as big as my pointer finger. He dipped the buckets into the tank and carried the fish to the edge of the water and dumped them in.

**To maintain pond health, as well as a viable stock of larger fish for catching, a pond is stocked carefully and monitored annually. A pond's size determines the ideal number of each species to add: Too many fingerlings add excess nitrogen to the water, and the limited food will prevent fish from reaching larger sizes. Too few predator fish, such as largemouth bass, and smaller fish will overtake the pond. "Undesirable" species, such as black crappie and carp, can multiply so quickly that few other fish will maintain a healthy breeding pool. Too few grass carp (a genetically engineered species that can't reproduce), and the pond can choke with algae and clog with vegetation.**

# Fishing

**The Bennett boys may not fish more often than many sport-loving kids, but they do have the opportunity to fish right where they live: at their pond, their neighbor's pond, or the nearby quarry or park. And unlike catch-and-release sportsmen, the Bennetts hope to catch enough fish for a real meal.**

**Cayne:** I'm probably the fisherman in the family. I like to eat the fish, but I like the challenge of catching them even more. Mostly, we catch bluegill, bass, and walleye. Our neighbors have bigger fish, because they have an old pond and we have a new one. Whenever we're on vacation, we take our fishing rods and find the best fishing place around there.

**Ali:** I catch fish by myself, too, but sometimes Dad or Caleb hooks one and I reel it in. Another way is if Dad throws in the line and then lets me hold the pole.

**Grey:** I'm the best fisher. No, Dad is, probably.

**Dad:** I dreamt of being a fisherman as a kid. But I only went once with my dad. And I didn't go hunting. So hunting and fishing became the big thing when I grew up.

**Grey:** For smallmouth bass, we use crawdads, and we can catch those in the creeks—about twenty are enough. For walleye, we use nightcrawlers.

**Cayne:** I like to use Catawba worms as bait. But I have to climb to find them, because they are always high up in a tree.

**Also known as catalpa worms, these caterpillars only feed on catalpa trees, devouring their leaves. Their scent attracts fish—especially catfish.**

**Caleb:** This is largest largemouth bass I've caught. It's from our neighbor's pond. Trust me, it was huge—at least six and a half pounds. I just used spinner bait. It was an old fish—a fish that had been in the pond maybe fifteen years—so you kind of hate to take a fish that old, a fish that was probably as old as I was at the time. So I let it go. The meat probably wasn't that sweet anymore, either.

**Chase:** They're actually caterpillars from the sphinx moth. And when you put them on a hook, they have this green ooze that attracts the fish.

**Caleb:** Dad said when he was a teenager, he'd just turn these worms inside out, and they'd last as long as you were fishing. I like to use top-water baits, like jitterbugs, that wiggle across the water. Right before dusk, a bass will come up right out of the water for these lures. We also like to use spinner lures.

Nightcrawlers are great, too. We used to place a sheet of plastic on the ground. It creates moisture, and the worms gather under it, so when you're ready to go fishing, you just lift the plastic, gather all the worms you need, and go.

**Grey:** And we always have a feast with whatever fish we catch. Dad and Caleb clean them all, and it takes a lot of fish, like a dozen or more, because our whole family loves fish. And Mom cooks. Or Dad will get out the big pot and deep fry the filets, which I really like, especially with tartar sauce.

The best of all ways to eat them is grilled in a wire basket over a campfire. Mom just puts a little lemon juice and salt and pepper on the fish, and they're awesome!

# Mushrooms

**Each spring, the Bennetts hunt for morels—or "mushrooms" as the locals simply call this one among the thousands of mushroom varieties that grow in this region. Whether black, gray, yellow, or blond, the morel's spongy, brain-like appearance is easily distinguished from the many poisonous or simply inedible mushrooms that can be found on rotting wood, forest floors, and fields from early spring to early winter.**

**Caleb:** We go looking from the middle of April through Mother's Day, depending on the amount of rain and the nighttime temperatures—oh, and luck!

**Dad:** Anymore, I don't really look anywhere but around dying elm trees—sometimes, near ash trees. Those are just the best bets for my time. But I know people who look under May apples, around apple trees, in areas that have been burned. And I figure that mushrooms need warmer soil, so where the sun can warm the forest floor is usually better.

**Chase:** If you can get Dad to go, he's the best. We'll be walking through the woods, and Dad will say, "Hey, what about those?" pointing right to where someone's about to step.

**Grey:** When you do find a mushroom, you get down low and wiggle it and try to leave the roots in the ground; that way, it will grow another mushroom.

**Although mushrooms don't have true "roots," Grey is right in that mushroom foragers usually cut free a mushroom in order to leave the bottom of the stalk intact. Some shake the spongy head hoping to dislodge the spores—they also ensure future mushrooms. The mushroom visible above ground is only the fruit of a complex fungus that lives beneath the surface.**

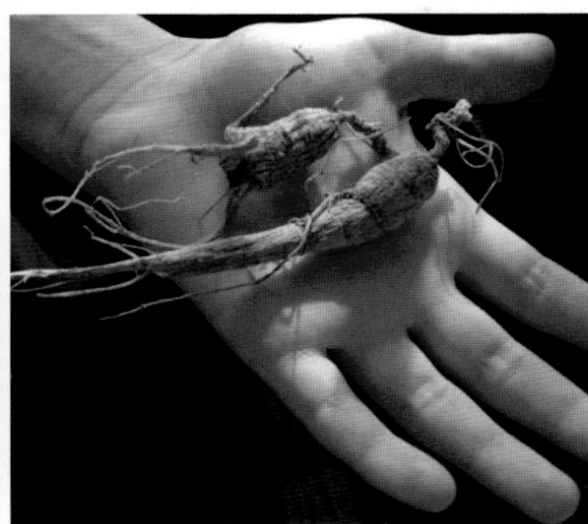

**Cayne:** There's one spot in the woods where Dad and Caleb found a bunch of mushrooms last year, so they marked it with some long, thin trees that were on the ground. We're hoping it will be a good spot for finding some again.

**Caleb:** We have found two or three mushrooms that were bigger than pop cans. That was back when I was young and Dad looked young.

**Mom:** I fry them up for the kids and Dad, but I got sick the first time I ate mushrooms, and I've tried them three other times. The last time I did, I threw up, and now that's it—I'm not eating any more.

**Caleb:** Not everyone loves them. I do. But I bet city kids would be shocked that kids go looking for mushrooms in the woods and then take them home and eat them fried up for breakfast or dinner.

**Chase:** If we find a whole lot, we can sell them. A few neighbors will pay maybe twenty dollars for a bread bag full of mushrooms. They are considered the most gourmet mushroom—even though they're just the ordinary one we have here—if we can find them.

**Chase:** The one other growing thing we hunt for is ginseng, which is worth a lot of money for a pound. (But you need to find a lot of ginseng roots to reach a pound once they're dried.) Dad's the best at finding this, too. You go looking in mid-summer, since the plants need to have three prongs coming out of the tuber, or else they're too small—and they're endangered, too, so you have to let them get big. And then they dry for a few months before you can sell them.

**Many Native American and Asian cultures consider ginseng *(Panax quinquefolium)* to be a plant with therapeutic and medical properties. For two centuries, this plant has been harvested and exported from Ohio and other nearby states; a pound of especially large roots currently sells for several hundred dollars. Yet this slow-growing plant, which requires between five and seven years to create a substantial root, has been so over-harvested that states now strictly regulate the plant's harvest. For instance, in Ohio wild specimens can only be collected between September and December if the plants have ripened berries and at least three leaf stems (prongs).**

# Summer

## by the Numbers

**50 to 70 chews**—the typical number of times a cow masticates (chews its cud) in a minute . . . while the typical human masticates 100 times in a minute of gum chewing (In 6 hours of daily eating, a cow chews at least 18,000 times—and offers up a considerable number of belches as well.)

**40 gallons**—amount of food and water a cow can hold in the first section of its stomach (It's like a vat full of enzymes that breaks down plant fiber and cellulose so that they can pass into the stomach's other three sections.)

**1,000 to 1,500 square bales**—number produced from the third (late-summer) cutting of the fields

**2,500 hours**—amount of time the newest tractor has been operated; the three others show more than 5,000 hours of use (Farm machines don't have odometers that tally the miles traveled. Instead, a machine's work is measured in hours.)

**–320°F**—the temperature of the liquid nitrogen in the canister in which the mail-order bull semen is stored

**2,000°F to 2,700°F**—the temperature of the hottest yellow and white flames burning the empty chicken coop

**4.5 miles**—length of an imaginary fire hose needed to bring water from the nearest fire hydrant to the Bennett's burning chicken coop

**8 owl decoys**—number that hang in the barn to keep birds from nesting inside

**40 nests**—average number of birds' nests in the barn during a year

**30,000 pounds**—amount of feed corn bought annually to feed out the barn cows and supplement the diet of the pastured cows

**800 kernels**—number of kernels found on an average ear of corn (typically in sixteen rows)

**20 quart bags**—amount of fresh sweet corn put up (frozen) by Mom and Ali this year

**65 quart jars**—amount of green beans put up (canned) by Mom and Ali this year

# Burning the Coop

**At the end of July, the new chickens are laying their first eggs—although the new nesting boxes, as well as the new coop with a concrete floor, have yet to be made. With the warm weather and the first days of swimming in the new pond, the Bennetts realized the old chicken coop—original to the farm and well beyond repair—blocked the view of the pond from the house.**

**"We had to burn it down because Mom couldn't see us when we were swimming," Ali explains. The laying chickens are moved to one side of the old double corncrib.**

**Chase:** We spent a little while clearing everything out of the coop—the chicken boxes and feeders and roosting ladders—and then Dad put diesel all over the building. (Diesel doesn't go up as fast as gasoline, so the fire spreads slowly.) And just as the roof started on fire, this huge black snake went flying down a roof beam and slithered off.

**Mom:** I'm sure the snake was sad to see its source of free eggs going up in smoke!

**Grey:** We started the fire just as the sun was going down, so as the sky got darker, the fire got brighter and brighter so you could walk around all night and see really well.

**Cayne:** The fire burned so hot, you couldn't even get close to it. We could watch from down by the pond or from up at the house. We threw sticks and stones into the fire, but it hurt your eyes if you looked at it too long—it was so bright. And the fire burned past midnight. When we walked there in the morning, you could suddenly see the pond from our porch. The ashes were still red and hot.

# Pond Swimming

**To visit a recreation center, public library, shopping center (with more than a handful of small storefronts), or many other facilities common to city life, residents of the area drive about twenty-five minutes to Zanesville or Newark. (Some residents do commute to Columbus or other metropolitan areas for work.) The new pond provides not only recreation, but also a place for swimming lessons.**

**Dad:** I learned to swim as a kid at the American Embassy in India. My family traveled a lot. We took the older boys for a few swimming lessons at the YMCA in Zanesville, but they really just taught themselves, starting with a swim vest—those bathing suits with a built-in life jacket—and noodles and inner tubes. And then they taught the younger kids.

**Ali:** I know how to swim a little. If I wear a life jacket, then I can use fins and swim. Dad is a good swimmer. So is Angus!

**Cayne:** The first time I swam in our pond, I had just learned how to swim. Now I can breathe underwater. With flippers I can outswim Caleb—barely. Probably my best thing is my back flip from the swing. Or even off the dock. The first time I think I just threw myself in backwards, diving, and then, eventually, I tried a real back flip and landed it. My dad knows how to do that, so I probably got the idea from watching him. But, really, I did the back flip on my second try. (I've done a few belly floppers since then, too.)

**Caleb:** In the middle of the summer, when you get in, the water feels like a hot tub. It's so hot, especially right on the top.

**Grey:** But other times, it's cold, and there's cold water underneath, like if you do a dive and go deep. Plus, you can open your eyes underwater and look for fish—it's pretty clear, but there aren't fish right where you are swimming. The bottom feels like you're stepping in a big pile of cow manure! But Dad did have sand and gravel put in on the swimming side of the pond.

**Chase:** Actually, when you're swimming or floating, you're not touching the bottom—only when you're climbing out—and if you use the ladder and the dock, you don't ever have to touch bottom. Plus it's really nothing more than squishy.

**Cayne:** The great thing about having a pool in your own yard is there are no other people crowding it. It's quiet, and you have all the space for playing water football or survivor-man, which is a game we invented where two of us try to get to home base while other kids try to tag us.

**Grey:** And your own pool is open all the time—as long as Mom and Dad say it is, and you aren't in trouble or anything and have to sit out.

# Pigs, Horses, and the County Fair

**For many locals, the Perry County Fair in New Lexington is the weeklong highlight of summer. The fair features demolition derbies; competitions in homemaking, art, and horticulture; displays by local organizations and youth groups; musical entertainment; typical rides and midway amusements; and a local favorite, the tractor tug pulls, in which various classes of old and new tractors see who can tow an increasingly heavy load the farthest distance before stalling or lifting their front wheels off the track.**

But the biggest focus is the showing and judging of livestock. In youth classes, area kids raise animals—either through FFA (Future Farmers of America) or 4-H Club programs—and compete for awards, trophies, and cash. Kids enter in their age divisions, as well as in animal-specific events that include goats, horses, lambs, chickens, rabbits, beef cows, dairy cows, and swine.

As Mom remembers, "We went every year when I was a girl, usually with the Girl Scouts because we had a booth there. I remember my mom always had us go through the cow barn—and I was always terrified of it! And here I am today with a cow barn of my own."

Caleb, age twelve, preparing to show his Hamp (short for Hampshire) pig, an all black pig with a white area across the top of the shoulders. This animal won "Swine Champion" in its weight class.

**Cayne:** We used to go to the county fair all the time, but now, that week is just about the only time we all have off between baseball all-stars and the start of football. I used to show pigs. In the winter,

you get a piglet that's maybe four months old—and then you take care of it and feed it until it gets to be like 250 pounds at fair time. Then you take it to the fair and walk in the judging ring where there's one other pig. Then the judges pick the best of that pair, and either you go on and meet the next pig, or you're out. If you've got one of the best pigs, you can sell it for a lot of money.

**Caleb:** We raised black-and-white Hamps (short for Hampshire), pinkish-white Yorkshires, and then a cross of those two pigs called Blue Butts—yes, that's their real name, because they're white with a grayish-blue rump.

**Chase:** My best year, I showed three pigs. So out of 250 entries, the judges take the top twenty to butcher, and then the rest of the judging goes by strict measurements of the meat and carcass. So I listened for the winners' names to be called, and when they got to the top ten, I thought maybe I'd missed my name. But then I was fourth place, out of all those entries. And Caleb got first in the weight class he was showing in. On top of that, of the two other pigs that I was showing, one took second place—that's class runner-up—and the other one took first. Finally, the judges take the best of all these classes to pick the grand champion. The judge looked at my one pig for so long, I thought I was close to winning.

**Caleb:** We'd go down to New Lex[ington] in our camper and stay there for a week so we could take care of our animals. The whole family would go. Chase and I would show two or three pigs each, and four or five times a day we'd feed and water them. You can't just dump a day's worth of food at once and let them eat a lot and get real big. They have to eat a little all day long so that they can look like a perfect picture of a pig for whenever a judge comes by.

**Mom:** We don't show calves, because if our boys were raising them in 4-H, and if we're raising calves on the farm to sell, people will wonder, "Well, are you showing your best calves at the fair, or are you keeping your best ones to feed out and sell later?"

**Cayne:** My favorite thing at the fair is this exhibit of the smallest horse and the biggest pig. They're kept in special pens, and you buy a ticket to go see them. I don't think they were raised around here.

# Getting Together

Getting together with friends and family, particularly in the warmer months, is the main social activity for the Bennett kids. Movie theaters, shopping malls, concerts, and dances—they don't seem to hold as much attraction, even though such things can be found within a twenty- or thirty-minute drive (if Caleb or one of the parents agrees to drive). Particularly because the work in the barn or the pastures often requires several hands, longer hours, or frequent checks, the farm itself is the "natural" setting for picnics, impromptu ball games, barbecues, camp-outs, and other casual events.

**Cayne:** Sometimes we get together with the Davy kids or another family for a clay pigeon shoot-out. Those are clay disks, not birds, that this launcher fires into the air, and you have to shoot so that the bullet shatters the disk; then you get a point. In a little tournament, each person gets like four shots (and I usually hit three). In a big tournament, maybe twenty-five clay pigeons are sent up for each shooter. Whoever busts up the most clay pigeons wins. Then afterwards, or maybe in the middle of the shoot-out, we have lunch or a fish fry.

**Mom:** People around here are just used to adding a few of the kids' friends at the last minute for a supper or having the kids spend the day or sleep over at someone else's house. Most of what I cook is pretty simple, done in a large quantity, and served family-style. And we usually eat a little later because

of the kids' practices and the fact that Dave and the boys usually work outside until dark. I often give the kids a snack earlier so we can all sit down later to a family meal.

**Chase:** Another thing we do is have campouts up on the hill, sort of at the back of our land. Bill loads up a wagon with hay, and people ride out and join us. We put up one big tent for our family, and the Davy family has a tent. We cook out and take the corn-hole boards back there. We have a big bonfire, and all us kids play hide-and-seek in the woods—or football or tag. Three or four times every summer we do that.

**Cayne:** Some kids probably pay to go away to summer camp to do things like hike in the woods, learn about nature, camp, cook on a campfire, swim, build stuff—things that we do on a regular day here at home.

**Grey:** Also, sometimes we kids and Dylan sleep out in the hayloft, especially if it's warm out. Once we were all up in the hayloft after dark, and all of a sudden, the lights went out. It was completely pitch-black dark. "Josh! Caleb! I know what you're doing!" I shouted out. But they weren't there. I went to flick on and off the light switch, but it didn't work. My friend Dylan jumped down from the hayloft—which is like fifteen feet!—and he landed and was up at the house before I was even out of the barn. I don't know how he could walk—that had to hurt his ankles! But it turned out that Dad and Dylan's dad had gone down to the basement of the house and turned off the lights in the barn from the fuse box, just to scare us as a joke.

**Similar to a game of horseshoes, corn-hole is a tournament where players toss objects (in this case, four bags filled with feed corn) to gain the most points by reaching the goal (in this case, a hole on one of two slanted boards set 30 feet apart). Players score 3 points for sinking a bag through the hole and 1 point for landing a bag on the board; the winner is the first to reach 21 points. While Cincinnati is considered the "home" of corn-hole, the game, also known as bean bag toss, baggo, or tailgate toss, is popular at family gatherings, fraternities, and parties in many states.**

Wild blackberry is one of several fruit-bearing brambles—prickly, shrubby plants in the rose family—that are common to the area. Because many birds and mammals feed on the berries that grow on each year's new canes, the seeds disperse very easily, giving the plants a reputation for being invasive.

## Growing Things

This year, the Bennetts are growing only one crop: alfalfa to feed their cattle and to provide some income from the sale of square bales; nothing for their own table. They are planning to add a large garden, which would require high fences to keep out the marauding deer, raccoons, rabbits, and ground hogs. "We used to grow our own corn—and tomatoes, green beans, and a few other things—but a vegetable garden ended up being 'just one more thing' on top of renovating the house, digging the pond, church, driving everyone where they need to be—and we have such good corn nearby, it seemed okay to let someone else grow it for a few years."

Having both grown up in the area, Mom and Dad know who else is growing corn, cucumbers, zucchini, beans, tomatoes, or green peppers. "People put in such large gardens around here," Mom says, "that they're grateful to have someone come get their extra harvest."

"I planted the sunflowers from seeds," says Ali. "And they grew taller faster than me—so then Mom had to lift me up to see them. We're letting the birds eat the seeds, but we could eat them if we wanted to."

**Mom:** And there's also the fun of picking wild fruit. When I was a little girl, my mother, my sister Alicia, and I always picked blackberries. There's nothing like wild blackberries in a pie. We've never planted a single cane here, and they come back year after year.

**Ali:** You have to wait for the fruit to turn from red to bluish-purple. But they have porcupine-things on the branches, and they can stick you.

**Cayne:** Most summers, we can pick enough blackberries behind the old corncrib and at the edge of the fields to make, like, eight pies. We froze enough this year to make six blackberry pies in the winter. On a really cold day, they'll be really good.

**Ali:** Green beans aren't wild like the berries. You have to plant green beans, and our friend Melvin did this year. Mom snaps the ends off, then I snap the beans in half. And then Mom boils them a little so they go into the jars that are in the boiling water. Now we have a cupboard that's full of jars that we can open later and don't have to go out and buy new green beans at the store.

**Chase:** Last year, Mom had a big cooler of unsnapped green beans—one of those big chests that you take camping. And I happened to be sick one day, so I was bored, and I snapped beans all day while I watched the History Channel.

# Fresh Corn

**Ali:** We always get corn from people around here. It's my favorite thing to eat. Usually I put too much salt on the cob because I put too much salt on everything (even though I know it's bad for me).

**Cayne:** Ted grows sweet corn for people like us, and he grows field corn, which is really hard and dry, just for cows. Other times we get corn from Cliff or Melvin, who live pretty near. I don't think we ever get it from the store.

I think everyone in the family is a typewriter corn-eater except Ali. She just takes a bite anywhere on the cob, then spins it, and eats another spot here or there. It makes us laugh.

**Ali:** I do not!

**Grey:** We save our corncobs. They either go to the chickens, which just peck at the cobs, or we break them in half and feed them to the cows. You can hold one in your hand, and they'll see it and come right over to take it. They are definitely not typewriter-eaters. They chew the cob in one bite!

# Summer Cows

**Caleb:** Come summer, the cows just graze. We keep them in one field until they've eaten down most of the grass, and then we move them to another field. If you ever want to see cows really move, just go stand near one of the gates that connects to the next pasture. I mean, the cows will go sprinting over and stand there bawling, waiting and hoping you'll open the gate.

**Dad:** "The grass is always greener" goes for the cows' way of thinking, too. You put them in one field, and if you're near another field, they suddenly want to be there. And then, if you bring them back into that field, in no time, they'll be wondering when they can go back through the gate to where they just were.

**Caleb:** In the spring, the grass grows faster, so it's thicker, and the cows can spend more time in one field. But in summer or fall, when the grass grows more slowly, we move the herd more. And they have access to the creek wherever we move them. They're fine on their own, but Angus checks in on them every day, just making sure.

# Breeding Cows

AI (no, the I does not stand for intelligence) is an abbreviation for Artificial Insemination. Insemination is the fertilization of an egg by a sperm. "Artificial" here means that the bull's sperm is injected into the cow by a trained breeder with a long syringe rather than by the bull itself.

**Chase:** When we first started out, a friend of ours had used some good bulls from this catalog that offers hundreds of bulls that can sire your calves. Now we've pretty much narrowed down our choices so we order semen from the same few studs every year. We can sell those AI-ed calves for a thousand dollars or more when it's a great cow with a stud whose name people recognize. Otherwise, when our own bull sires the calf, five or six hundred dollars is pretty typical for a calf.

Our #10 has a calf that's probably worth two thousand dollars today. But we're keeping her and her calf, too, so that both can have another calf.

We AI our best cows, and the bull takes care of others. As a cow comes into heat, we separate her from the herd, wait twelve hours, and then AI her. We can let her back out into the pasture as long as the bull is nowhere near. If the AI takes, that cow won't come into heat again that season. But if it doesn't take, she'll come back into heat in twenty-one days.

As for the cows we're not AI-ing, our bull knows when they're in heat, and he doesn't have any competition since we have just one mature bull.

We try to plan it so that most of the births come out in the spring and early summer. If we're calving in March and April, there's the nice growth of the first grass, which is better for the mother who has to feed both herself and her calf.

To AI a cow, we need Ray. He's the one who's certified and trained to do this. He and Dad bought the gomer bull together, and now Ray's like a family friend. But when he comes over and starts setting up, we always like to kid him . . .

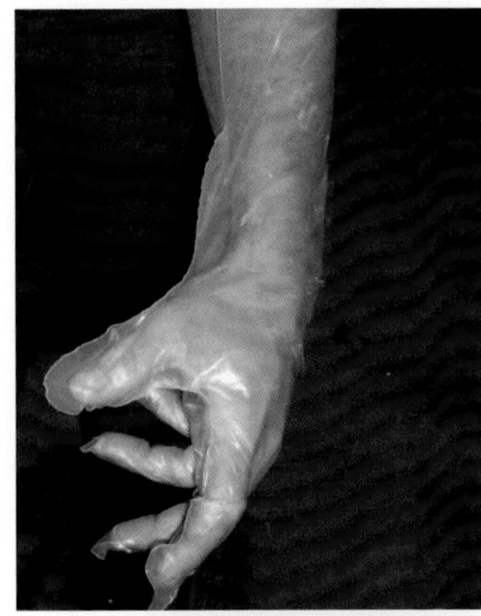

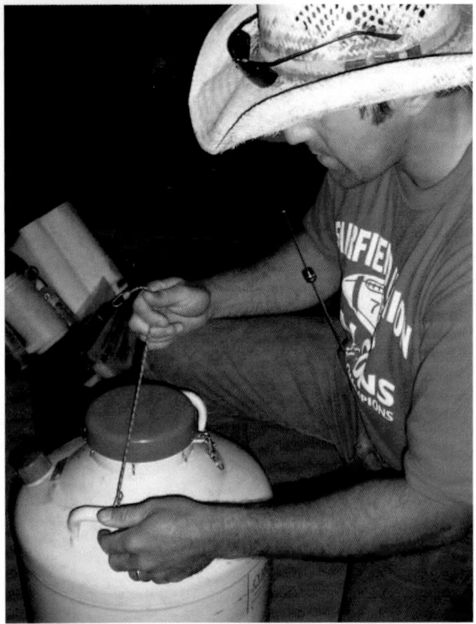

**Cayne:** "Hey cows! Guess who's here? Your boyfriend Ray!"

**Grey:** "Hey, Ray, that cow told me she loves you, you best of all!"

**Caleb:** We all joke around with Ray because he's got the amazing job: part veterinary science, and part . . . you know. But none of us is trained to do what he knows how to do.

**Chase:** You don't really know what time Ray is going to come. We're just one of the farms he visits; he probably tends a hundred cows. So sometimes, he comes during the day, but a lot of the time, it's late, or really late and completely dark when Ray gets here.

**Dad:** Twelve hours after the cow will stand—that means she's receptive to breeding—it's time to AI her. Generally, our cows come into heat late evening or early morning. So if they'll stand about dawn, Ray comes that evening. And if they'll stand in the evening, Ray will come in the morning.

**Cayne:** Basically, Ray brings a canister that's smoking-cold with liquid nitrogen. It holds the straws of semen we ordered from the catalog. He warms it up in water that's about the cow's inside temperature.

**Grey:** Then he puts on a long plastic glove that covers his whole arm and he comes out to where we've got the cow in the head gate: That's the chute that ends in a two-door gate with a round hole in the center that holds the cows head in place so she can't back out. And then Ray reaches in—he has to remove the cow poop from inside her so he can AI her. That's not as gross as it sounds: The cow poop is everywhere else around here, so it's nothing new.

**Dad:** What Ray explained, is that he feels for the ovarian tract through the cow's rectum. He inserts the straw into the cow's vagina until it reaches the cervix. He can feel the tip of the straw pass through three rings, and once it's there, past the third ring, he presses on the syringe on the end of the straw to deposit all the sperm right where an egg can be fertilized.

**Chase:** The whole thing takes maybe five to ten minutes, and then the cow's done! It doesn't hurt them at all. In fact, the cow usually just stares or nibbles some grain while it's happening.

# Milk Cows

**This summer, the Bennett farm grew by two dairy cows acquired from a nearby family. "Dairy farmers usually get rid of their bulls immediately," Caleb explains. "They sell them to people who will raise them for meat, because dairy farmers can't have the calves drinking milk from their mothers—that's the milk they want to bottle!—and the males aren't going to end up giving milk themselves. So we knew a family that had two calves this year, and we thought we'd get them for the younger kids to raise."**

**Chase:** The two dairy cows were handfed before we got them. That sounds like they were fed hands, and they do like to suck on your hand if you let them.

**Cayne:** If you have your hand in an animal's mouth, you just think you're going to get bit. But these calves don't have teeth when they're young like this.

**Grey:** "Handfed" just means they know how to suck from a bottle instead of their mother's udder. So now we have to feed them with a huge milk bottle filled with formula about two times a day. We're their mother. Mom or Dad mixes up this special powdered milk with water, and then we can feed it to the two cows.

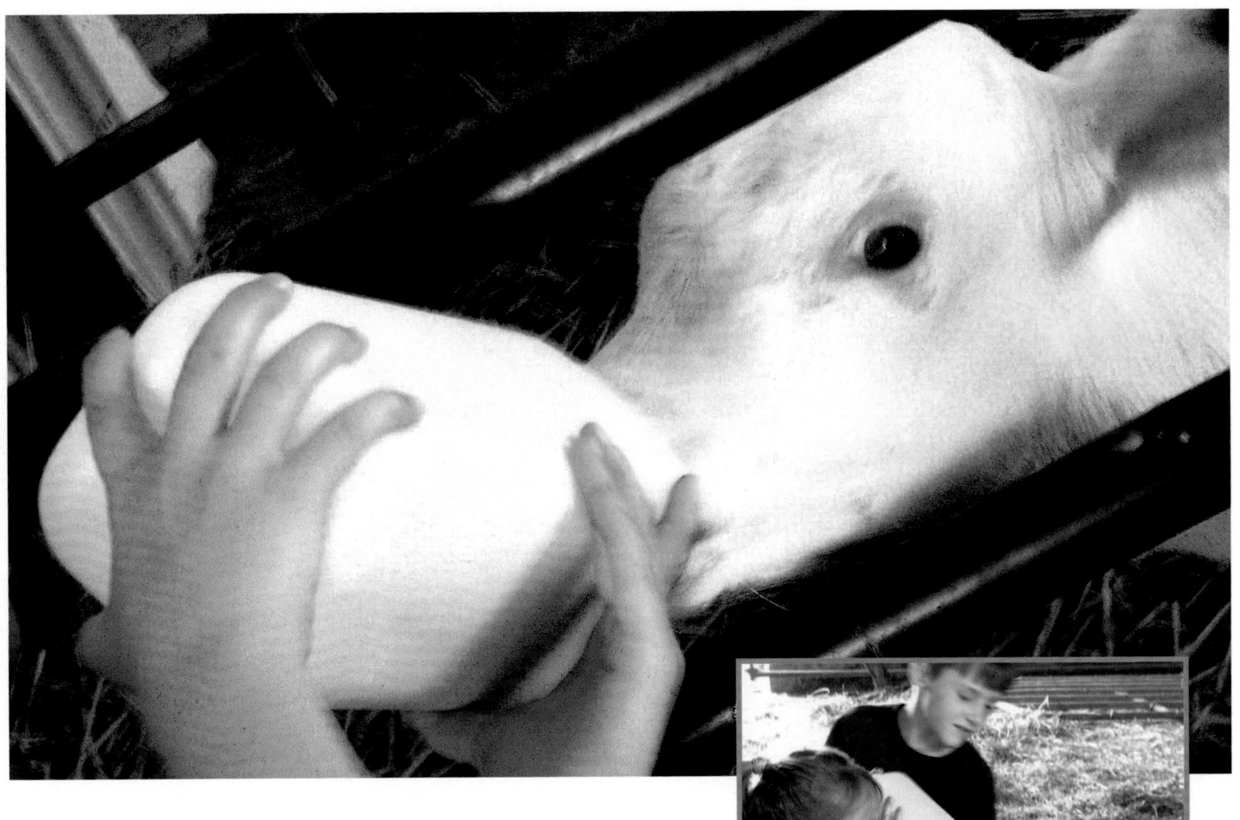

**Ali:** The bottle is too heavy to lift myself, but I can hold it with someone else. The cows make this sucking sound... *shchpt... shchpt... shchpt...* when they are drinking, and their eyes are different from the other cows': They're pink and bluish and brownish—and brighter than the Angus cows'—maybe because their faces are white.

**Caleb:** What happened is that those two cows just aren't afraid of us. When you raise calves from such a young age, they get so used to you that they're sort of annoying—always in the way, instead of moving out of the way if you have to get something or move them from one corral to another.

Very quickly, the Jersey calves will learn to drink their formula from buckets, rather than bottles. The calves are then weaned onto grain by mixing the dried corn with the formula in the shallow bucket; slurping the milk, the cows will swallow grain as well. Gradually, the calves will be fed separate buckets of water and grain.

# Angus, Angus

Working alongside the tractors one particularly hot summer day, Angus, the border collie, suffered a major stroke. Exhaustion, dehydration, something else—the Bennetts will never really know—triggered a stroke that paralyzed the lower half of the dog's body. He could neither stand nor walk. His suffering was immediately obvious to everyone.

Each member of the family felt Angus's loss in a profound way. For the three youngest children, Angus had been a central feature in every memory of their life on the farm. For the two older boys, Angus had accompanied them anywhere they'd ever been on the farm: He shadowed their work, raced ahead of their steps, became as much a part of their view as the horizon.

But perhaps Angus's loss was hardest for their father. Angus had been his constant helpmate, working the cattle day and night with or without him. Angus responded to the sound of that man's voice as keenly as he did the bleating of a calf or the bellowing of a cow.

**Grey:** When Angus was dying, he took his front legs—that was all that could move—and climbed up onto my dad's feet, but he was looking over at the cows, down at a new calf, and my dad knew he wouldn't ever be able to see the cows again.

**Dad:** Angus lived for those cows. He wouldn't have been Angus without working his cows.

**Grey:** That's how we knew it was the end.

**Caleb:** We buried the dog on our property. It was pouring rain. Chase and I dug a grave, and our shovels stuck in the mud, sucking each time we lifted up some earth. We buried him in one of the blankets he used to sleep on. And we're planting a tree over the top of the site.

**Six weeks after Angus's death, the family acquired a border collie puppy from an Ohio breeder. "We named him Angus, too," Ali explains, "because he's going to work with our cows again, and they're all Angus cows!"**

## Square Baling

**Chase:** At the third cutting, we make a lot of square bales because we can sell these. They go for up to four dollars a bale, and people who buy them need like sixty or ninety bales. Normally we sell grass hay, which isn't as rich as alfalfa hay. You can't afford to sell bales for much less because it costs to make the bales: diesel fuel for the machines, plus Dad pays us sometimes, too, for helping.

**Dad:** When it's perfect hay, we make square bales. At about seventy pounds, they're easier to move around and more valuable per pound. But I don't want to be hauling dozens of square bales out to feed our cows. Now round bales weigh a thousand pounds, but they only sell for twenty-five dollars; so it's best to keep those for feeding our animals. But square bales, even with that extra labor, are a lot more valuable.

**Chase:** We add potash to the alfalfa field every year, because that's what alfalfa takes out. And we add lime every few years. And we didn't get as much alfalfa this year, which is normally about 120 round bales. We need a round bale and a quarter every day—nine bales a week—to get our herd through the year.

**Caleb:** So square baling is just a different last step from round baling. A different machine makes the final shape. The square baler picks up the raked hay and pushes it through this square tunnel. When there's enough hay compacted there, strings wrap around and secure the bale. Finally, the bale travels down a short conveyor and, when it reaches

the end, it triggers a spring that flings the bale toward the wagon where Josh and I stack start stacking bales in rows. You want to get as many bales as possible onto the wagon.

One day this summer, I got on the tractor at nine in the morning, and I literally didn't get off it until 10:30 at night—I ate lunch on the tractor. But we had hay to cut and bale in a couple of the fields—we were trying to beat the weather—so even though that was one of my only days off school, I spent thirteen hours mowing, tedding, raking, baling . . .

**Cayne:** I do some square baling. I can catch a bale, but not in midair the way Caleb and Josh can, but I can make sure the bale doesn't land the wrong way and bounce off. And then I can drag the bales over to where they have to be stacked. It's easier if you pull a bale up to your chest and walk with it. There's a lot of dust and straw that gets all over you, so afterward, you just want to jump in the pond.

**Caleb:** I figure that Josh and I each lift about 210,000 pounds in about one month of square-baling. That's two thousand bales, about seventy pounds apiece, with each bale getting lifted three times: once onto the wagon, once up to the hayloft, and once over to wherever we're stacking. So each of us lifts about 105 tons!

# Fall

## by the Numbers

**100 pounds**—amount of Concord grapes harvested from the Bennetts' three plants

**28 jars**—amount of Concord grape jelly put up by Mom and Ali

**6 to 8 months**—time until a calf is weaned from its mother

**10 to 12 months**—time it takes to feed out a cow in the barn before butchering

**37 cows**—number from the Bennett farm sold at the fall livestock auction

**1,000 to 1,250 pounds**—average weight of an eighteen to twenty-two-month-old cow brought to market (Less than half of a live steer's weight will end up as "retail cuts" of meat, such as steaks, roasts, or ground beef. For instance, a 1,200-pound steer yields between 435 and 518 pounds of meat, depending on its grade.)

**2 to 4 pounds**—average weight an Angus cow gains each day as it's fed out for slaughter

**600,000 deer**—estimated population living in Ohio in 2006

**4,838 deer**—animals harvested in the 2006 hunting season just in Perry County (Throughout the state, slightly more than one-third of all deer were taken by hunters—1,749 were antlered; 2,989 were non-antlered, meaning does and males with small "button" antlers shorter than three inches.)

**66,626 youth hunters**—number of kids 17 and under licensed for the 2006 Ohio deer season

**18 pounds**—average weight of a male wild turkey (Hens only weigh about 8 pounds; hunting them is not permitted.)

**5,100,000 to 5,300,000 wild turkeys**—number of the Eastern subspecies of this bird in the United States (About two million wild turkeys of other subspecies make up the U.S. total turkey population of about seven million—from a mere thirty thousand in the early 1900s, when they were hunted nearly to the point of extinction.)

# School

The Bennetts attend schools in the Northern Local School District, which serves about 165 square miles. It contains three elementary schools, including Glenford, which the younger Bennetts still attend, and Sheridan Middle and High schools. (High schools in the state capital, Columbus, draw students from five or ten square miles.) Approximately 97 percent of the students in the county are white; almost 60 percent are of German or English descent. Eighty percent of the 750+ students finish high school, and 20 percent go on to attend a two- or four-year college.

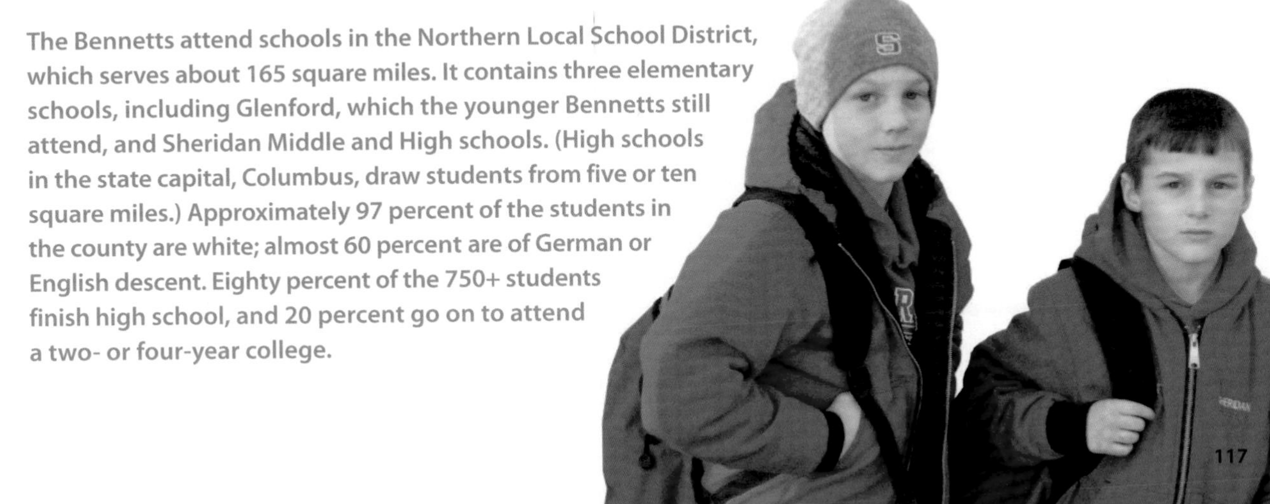

**Because many families rarely leave the area, field trips—especially in elementary school—offer experiences beyond what the county provides. Day trips to Columbus or Zanesville might include a visit to a conservatory, arboretum, zoo, arts or science center, or even The Wilds wildlife refuge.**

**Cayne:** Mom drives Grey and me to school. We leave about 8:50, and school starts at 9:00. Then we ride the bus home. I'm maybe the sixth person off, so I'm home in ten minutes, around 4:00. But lots of kids have longer rides, in the morning and after school—maybe like an hour.

**Grey:** I know at least one kid in my grade—well, he's actually the principal Mrs. Gussler's son—who has to get up at 6:30 to get to school, because they drive from New Lexington, and Mrs. Gussler has to be here a long time before school starts.

**Cayne:** Some kids stay on for the after-school program, and their parents pick them up even later. But Grey and I get home in time to grab a snack, do homework maybe, then play outside for a while if it's nice, and then we'll go to football practice or a game. Dad's the coach, so he takes us, and we're home a little before eight for dinner together.

But we have the same subjects as kids who live in a bigger city. We go shopping for the same school supplies and school clothes. In some cities kids walk to school or walk home for lunch, but here, only a

few kids live close enough to school to walk, and everyone eats in the cafeteria.

**Chase:** What's different about schools out here? One thing isn't different: kids not from here might think we're all a bunch of farm hicks who don't care about learning and only get by so we can go home to our cows. But Sheridan, my school, has scored among the top Ohio schools in the proficiency tests. For instance, in Caleb's class, four girls graduated with a perfect 4.0—all four years.

**Caleb:** My class has 81 percent of the kids going to college—we have the most in the school's history.

**Chase:** And Caleb almost had a 4.0 himself—he got a few As and one B—believe it or not, in Ag! Agriculture! They dropped him one whole letter grade because he didn't have a signature on some paper.

**Caleb:** That was ridiculous. I had finished keeping this log about pigs, figuring up how much I had in feed, how much in time, and so on, showing whether or not it makes business sense to raise your own pigs. Dad and I were going over my report, and he just forgot to sign it—I thought he had. So I got docked for not having the signature. That was enough Ag for me—that one year.

With Caleb (above in white), a three-year varsity-team wrestler as their coach, Cayne and Grey practice or compete at Sheridan High School two or three times every week throughout autumn and winter.

**Chase:** And I'm not planning to take any Ag. I've learned most everything from Dad already. Anyway, that's one difference about Sheridan and schools in a city. We have Ag Ed where you learn basic farming stuff. The kids join Future Farmers of America and study practical things like repairing machines, animal nutrition—but, I don't know, I think kids in my class are more business-oriented, so even if they take Ag, they might not go into farming as a career.

I will probably have at least a small farm, whatever I do, wherever I end up living. It takes a good bit of work, but it's rewarding.

**Grey:** Most of our friends don't have farms like ours, but a lot of them do have one animal they're raising for the 4-H Club. Some of them, like Colin's family, grow vegetables. His family raises a lot of vegetables, and they have cows, too.

**Chase:** One funny thing. When we go to the state football tournaments, we always see kids from private schools or wherever with letter jackets that have all kind of pins on them we've never seen, like bowling and speech and glee club and other activities we don't have. At Sheridan, we have football and golf in fall—and volleyball for girls, which is really popular; wrestling and basketball in winter; and baseball and track in spring. And maybe five kids do swimming, and they travel all the way to the YMCA in Zanesville for practices.

**Sheridan High School offers three courses in Agricultural Education, covering animal science, woodworking, soils, small engines, welding, farm equipment, livestock health, and other topics, many of which involve home projects and hands-on experience.**

**Cayne:** Another difference is our Thanksgiving break; we get Thursday through Monday off, Monday being the first day of shotgun season.

**Caleb:** I think it's not the academic part, but the social time that's probably unique about living out here. The only gatherings, the only things to do for high-school kids, are school sport events and school dances. Sports are huge. I remember we hosted a play-off game my sophomore year, and there were three thousand people at the high school. Weekends, kids just go to someone's house to hang out, or we meet up at school for a match, ball game, wrestling meet —or girls' volleyball is also great, especially for meeting girls.

It's not like we hang out at restaurants, at malls, or on college campuses. We've got each others' houses or the concession stands at school events. They'll bring in local pizza. They'll have sweet stuff and drinks, but for us, for a family of seven, if everyone wants something, that can be expensive. So for wrestling, especially since we're there from nine until nine, the mothers will get together and make sloppy joes or shredded-chicken sandwiches or figure out a potluck so all the kids can eat whenever during the day. Kids and families—teachers, sometimes—they're all at school, hanging out for the day.

**Chase:** Schools really are the community center.

# Grapes

**Farm life hardly takes into account summer vacation, which barely lasts twelve weeks. The first day of school is in late August. Like kids most everywhere in America, the Bennetts spend as much of the last warm days and bright evenings outside. So, in addition to homework and after-school practices or games, they still have cows to feed, fields to mow, and, suddenly, a huge crop of ripened Concord grapes to harvest.**

**Ali:** I cut grapes that are down low, and then someone drives the skid steer, and Mom and Caleb climb in the bucket. It lifts them up to get the higher grapes. Cutting the stems is a little hard for me, but not for the boys. I think it took seven of us one hour to get all the grapes. Plus, we ate some, too.

**Chase:** I bet we picked about a hundred pounds —three full buckets. Every year we do that.

**Ali:** Once they're in buckets, we take them down to the basement. Then we all have to wash our feet real well and carry each other downstairs so we can stomp the grapes. All the grapes are in big buckets. I climb into one and just start stepping, and the grapes pop and shmoosh between my toes. After a few minutes of stomping, it's someone else's turn. My feet weren't purple when I was done, except for little pieces of grape skin on them.

Grapeseed oil, as well as various chemical compounds in grape skins, is used in cosmetics to create a smoother complexion by sloughing off dead skin cells and stimulating new cell growth. Pummeling grapes with your feet is much harsher than gently dabbing or scrubbing your skin with a cream containing grape extracts. This results in the itchy skin that grape stompers often experience.

**Grey:** But your feet do end up feeling itchy—for maybe a couple of days afterwards. I don't know why, so Mom does most of the stomping until all the grapes are crushed and juicy.

**Chase:** Then the crushed grapes rest a few days in this special bucket that has slits in the bottom. It's like a press, because you can crank the wood lid onto the grapes and press out all the juice. Dad thought he would try to make wine with some of the grapes, and Mom and Ali make jelly.

Supposedly, it takes a long time for grapes to turn to wine. Over several months, you have to stir it. We all get to taste a little while it's still just grape juice with sugar. So far, it tastes pretty much like melted grape jelly.

**Ali:** For making jelly, we have this giant cone, and it has a little baseball bat that squishes the grapes when you push it in a circle. All the juice goes out the little holes in the cone, but the seeds can't get out.

Mom does the rest of the jelly-making, because the jars are in boiling water, and the juice is cooking on the hot stove. But I add the sugar, stir sometimes, and keep her company. We've also made strawberry, blackberry, blueberry—and I-forget-what-else jelly.

# Cows in the Fall

**Caleb:** Getting the cows off to auction, we first herd them all into the barn. We move the animals into a smaller pen and then separate out the calves. Then we sort them and decide who will be in the herd. Just a long piece of plastic pipe and yourself is all you need to get them moving. They just move away, move away from you, and generally stay in one group. But that does make it hard to get one particular cow that you might want from the middle of the crowd.

**Dad:** We're selling thirty-seven calves at the auction this year. Every animal that wasn't AI-ed, and that we aren't planning to eat, is going. The elite ones, the AI-ed cows, we're selling to people who are probably going to breed them or take them to the fair. The rest were bought to feed out and eat.

All the cows we're keeping have given birth, and all of them have been bred back to the bulls. And we're fattening up two or three.

**Caleb:** We go half an hour from here to the Muskingham Livestock Sale. It has all these seats that surround a pen. Each auction starts with an announcer who says the bidding will start at however-much-per pound, and then he adds facts like what the animal weighs, breeding information, stuff that impresses buyers.

**Dad:** They sell something like 1,200 or 2,000 cattle every week, year round. But they also sell sheep, goats—all kinds of livestock.

**Caleb:** So we drop off the cows, and then we have breakfast and listen for how the first few animals sell. Then we're pretty much done with our part. A couple of days later, we get a check for what all the animals sold for, minus the little commission the auction house takes. Whoever ends up buying animals loads them up and takes them from there.

Dried corn is considered the least expensive and most available source of calories: the more calories, the more a cow will weigh at auction. Weight can literally "tip the scales" from a cow selling at a loss to a cow selling at a profit.

**Dad:** The unpredictable thing is that one year a cow might bring seven hundred dollars, and that very same cow, if it were another year, might bring twelve hundred dollars. No difference in the animal. No difference in what we did raising it. Only difference: the price of corn. And the push to turn corn into ethanol for fuel has certainly driven up corn prices.

Now some farmers are having their cows spend more time in the pasture, eating grasses, and less time in the barn being fed corn. But grass-fed beef is another taste, and, at least locally, buyers want the fattier, corn-fed animals. So if corn goes up to something like four dollars a bushel, the cost of feeding that cow is going to be high, and there would be no profit in a seven-hundred-dollar sale, so the animal sells for the twelve-hundred-dollar price. And when the price of corn falls, it's going to be less expensive to feed an animal, so it's not going to bring in twelve hundred dollars.

Year to year, we just have no way of knowing. We just breed our best animals and hope for the best sales at the auction.

**Caleb:** Normally, we send two or three cows to the butcher each year. One cow pretty much takes care of us. The rest of the meat, Dad can sell. And then we keep the meat from two or three deer we kill, and maybe we give another one or two deer to our relatives and family friends.

# Beef

Several days after the Bennetts deliver the cows to the local meat processing plant—a short five-minute drive away—the meat is ready for pick-up, neatly wrapped in individual sheets of white butcher paper and labeled "hamburger," "T-bones," "stew meat," and so forth.

A typical Angus cow yields less than half its weight for the table. Its carcass is butchered into several sections. Starting on the top, going from neck to tail, there is the chuck, muscular flavorful meat that requires slower, moist preparation; the rib; the short loin and the sirloin, which include the choicest cuts such as T-bones, porterhouse steaks, and the filet mignon; and the round, the large and lean rear section and top of the hind leg. Along the cow's underside, from chest to belly, there are the brisket and the fore shank, which are both slow-cooked to make them tender; the short plate, used mostly for stew meat; and the flank, which is lean muscle usually sliced thinly against the muscle fibers.

**Caleb:** We load the fattened cows in our red trailer and leave them at Cotterman Brothers. They have a holding pen inside their barn where all the animals get tagged (so they'll know which animal belongs to which family). Once a week, I think, all the animals are, you know, slaughtered, frozen and—well, it's all the stuff that people don't want to know about. But it's how the meat gets the size to fit on the dinner table.

**Chase:** And the almost-empty freezer is instantly full. Everything ready to cook. Ted also butchers sheep, pigs—he does a lot of the fair pigs—and lots of what hunters like us bring in during deer season.

**Mom:** Growing up, I ate what my mom put on the table, but I didn't really know much about cooking myself. But being a mom out here? I have learned! Honestly, I'd never actually touched raw meat until I got married. I had my hands in plastic bags the first time I cooked hamburgers, and Dave walked in. "What are you doing?" he shouted, laughing. So I got over that.

**Cayne:** I like steaks cooked until not all the juices are gone, but they're still really tender. Maybe with pepper on it sometimes, or steak sauce. Tenderloin is always the best.

I don't ever think that we're eating the cows that we raised. I guess if someone stopped me at dinner and said, "Do you realize you're eating that cow, you know, #7 or #8?"—maybe that would be weird.

**Mom:** The only thing we get from the butcher that's sort of different is ox tail, which is the cow's tail, and some people won't eat it because, well, they know where it was. But I make an ox-tail soup with lots of vegetables that's really rich, and the kids love it.

# Hunting Seasons

At times—and certainly hunting is the most dramatic moment—country life can appear to be centuries away and worlds apart from modern city life. Yet every meal enjoyed in the city depends on the work enjoyed or endured in the country. Whether hunting for food or driving to the supermarket, it's the same idea in both cases: providing nutritious food to hungry people as economically as possible.

For the Bennetts, hunting is also a skill to master akin to a great lay-up shot on a basketball court, a take-down move on a wrestling mat, or a back flip off the dock. It's a bond that's shared between generations—a sort of coaching or mentoring that provides an ongoing sense of pride and accomplishment. "Hunting is also part of being a responsible caretaker," Dave explains. "As long as we're living here, we have to manage the wildlife and forests on our property—it helps take care of us, and we help take care of it."

**Dad:** Plenty of times, when it's dark, we'll ask who wants to go on a coon hunt. Even Ali joins in. When she sees the coon in the tree, she gets so excited that Duke got another coon. That's his job, and the kids love that. I can see that kids in town maybe won't understand that. I mean, show me a family where you'd find an eighteen-year-old and his four younger siblings all together on a Friday night, going out with their hound, and having a great time together just looking for raccoons. I guess it's rare these days for a whole family—teenagers and younger kids—all having dinner together with their parents, and then staying in just to play a game or watch a movie. I feel we're lucky to have this life.

**Caleb:** It's true, I don't really like driving or going all that far. I've been to Buckeye Outdoors—that's about twelve miles from here. But I haven't wanted to drive much beyond that.

**Chase:** I know some people think of hunters as people who buy guns and go out, all trigger-happy, to start shooting at whatever moves. Nothing could be farther from the truth. Take me, for instance: I'm fifteen, and I just now started hunting by myself. You have to wait until you're older, so you can understand more about hunting and don't make a mistake. You need guidance.

My dad's big on safety. He got shot in his shoulder when he was younger—he and a friend were just looking at a gun indoors—and it went off. We still have his shirt with the bloodstain and the tear from when the doctors ripped the shirt to treat him. I took it for show-and-tell one year in elementary school, just to show how safe you have to learn to be.

# Turkeys

The turkey and the Moscovy duck are the only two birds domesticated in the New World. European explorers found turkeys in Mexico and brought them home to Europe in the early 1500s, where they thrived. When the English returned to America to settle the northeastern seaboard, they brought "their" turkeys with them. Today, domestic turkeys sport the white-tipped tail feathers of their Mexican ancestors. The tails of actual wild turkeys have chestnut-brown tips.

**Chase:** We usually go turkey hunting in the spring and fall. Wild turkeys, which are huge, are nothing like the birds raised for Thanksgiving. You can find wild turkey tracks in the snow—or you can find turkey feathers. But turkey hunting is a lot harder than hunting deer or rabbit or coon. We have plenty of wild turkeys on our land, but Caleb's only ever killed, like, two. And Dad's only killed one here. You have to wear tons of camouflage—even on your hands and face. If a turkey senses one thing is wrong, it's gone. Your best chance of shooting a turkey is when it's walking on the ground. But shooting them is different.

**Dad:** Once I did kill three turkeys with two shots—one flew right behind another one just as I was getting off a shot. But that was an accident! When you're hunting turkeys, you need to remember one thing: A turkey's eyesight is phenomenal. As my mentor John Campbell was fond of saying, "To a deer, every hunter is log. To a turkey, every log is a hunter."

**Caleb:** You only eat the breast meat of wild turkeys—the legs have too many tendons. They are tough as wires. But, if I remember, they're delicious.

# Deer

**Chase:** When deer are mating—"in the rut" is what it's called—hunting season starts. It's when the bucks are fighting to see who is strongest and who gets to mate with the does. Some hunters put out deer decoys near their stand. Some use these hunting cans that make a sound that imitates the bleating of a doe when you turn the can over. And that attracts bucks. Some hunters take two deer antlers or metal sticks and beat them together to sound like bucks butting heads. Older bucks grow smarter each year. If they've been shot at, they get harder to catch.

On the first day of shotgun season, everyone goes hunting, so all the schools are closed. You wake up at five in the morning, or you go out two hours before it gets dark. (There are hunters who stay out all day and sit for a long, long time.) Sometimes groups of people go out, and some will go through the woods, trying to drive the deer out, while other guys are waiting right where the deer are heading—they hope. But we mostly hunt from tree stands. Maybe on the last day of the season, if someone hasn't got his deer, we'll work together and drive the deer out, making noise and all.

We also hunt deer during bow season. It's around the start of October and stays on until January. But if I go, I only get off one shot—I just don't have the strength to pull back the bowstring and reload. So I've got to make one good shot, or else get some help to reload.

**Grey:** I was in the newspaper when I shot my first deer, because I was only six and most kids are in third or fourth grade when they get their first deer. When you're little, you normally shoot for a doe—since you're hunting for meat. I was with my dad on one of our deer stands, this big tree with some nailed-up boards that makes a ladder. When I saw the doe, it was about ten yards away, and I hit her on the first shot. It was the first time I'd used a gun, except for a BB gun. Dad taught me things like how you line up the deer in the V of the sights. I killed it right away—it ran a little bit, but then just dropped.

We went to get the truck so we could take the deer and gut it. (I don't do that because the knife is really sharp.) Then it goes to the tagging station, like Steve's store, so he can record that we got a deer.

Ted made me this lamp with the four legs from my first doe. You don't mount the head of does, since they don't have the racks. But does taste better, even if they don't have as much meat as bucks. We usually freeze the meat right away, and then give it to Ted, and he makes deer jerky for us. I eat that for snacks sometimes. It looks just like meat, but it's hard and sliced real thin. And spicy! I usually get a glass of water before eating some.

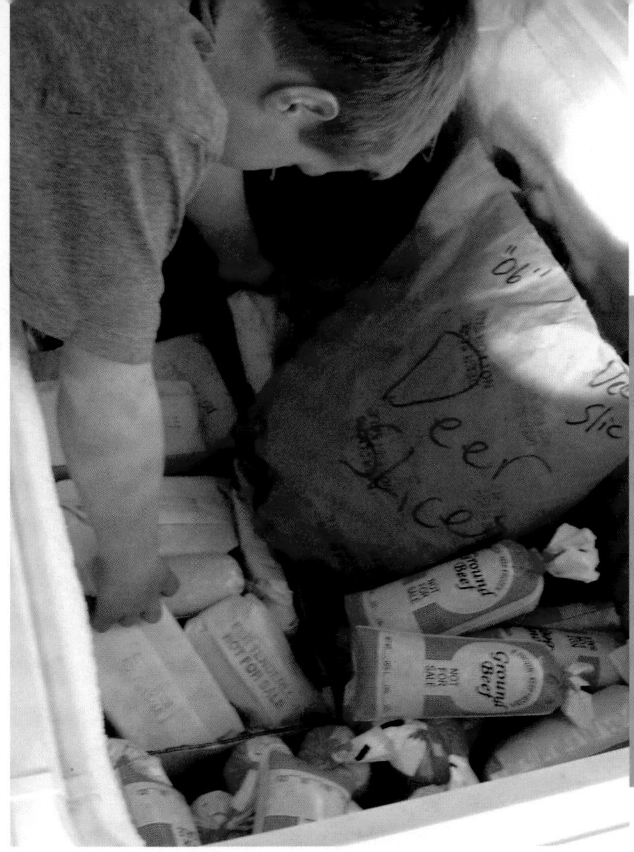


**Chase:** We get tenderloin from the deer, sometimes butterfly-shaped, and Mom will fry them or grill that. And we get ground-up meat that she makes into sauces or meat loaf. You can use that just to make burgers, but it's a little grittier, and it doesn't taste the same as cow meat, so we usually mix it with some ground beef.

**Chase:** Since I was about nine, I've killed one buck and one doe each year—that's what the state usually lets each person do. Caleb gets about the same, but he doesn't go for any buck that isn't bigger than the one he's shot previously. And Dad rarely gets a buck, because he only wants to get a big deer with a rack with something like ten points. Their standards are higher than mine—for now.

**Grey:** This one guy got a buck with a 28-point rack. I think it had a few stickers. (A point has to be at least one inch long; any bump on the antler that's smaller than that is called a sticker.)

We wear clothes so other hunters see that we're out. All orange. See, deer hunters just look for things that are moving, and you don't want to wear brown and just blend into the woods. Deer are color blind, so they don't see how bright orange we are.

Before I killed my first buck, I saw this huge twelve-point buck, but Dad didn't let me shoot at it because it was too far away. You don't want to injure a deer, because they get injured for their whole life. So you don't make a stupid shot. If you don't hit them right behind the front shoulder—where the lungs and heart are—they'll get away.

In the 1900s, half a million white-tailed deer (*Odocoileus virginianus*) roamed the United States. Current estimates put their number as high as thirty million. The overpopulation of deer prevents forests from regenerating (saplings are a favorite food); the timber industry reports a $750 million loss annually from the deer's voracious feeding. Deer devour underbrush, which eliminates the habitats of other wildlife. And deer cause traffic accidents, costing $8 billion in some two million accidents each year—that's a 50 percent increase in the last fifteen years.

**Chase:** This farmer near us had so many deer that were destroying his crop that he was allowed to hunt even before hunting season officially began. He got a special nuisance permit. We don't have corn, but the deer do eat our alfalfa hay and bed down out there. Deer are just a part of life out here. Deer put food on our table—just like cows—except cows you have to buy and feed and care for, and then you have to pay to have them butchered, so all that makes them a lot more expensive to eat.

**Dad:** When I was young, I could hardly sleep the night before deer season opened. I so anticipated that morning. No school. The first chance to go out. But I think a lot of people think hunters don't like deer—or whatever animal they're hunting. But I have a great respect for these animals. Yes, there are too many deer—the herd needs to be thinned. But I don't want any animal to suffer. I want a clean shot that drops the animal quickly. And we eat almost everything we kill—sharing the meat with friends and family.

# The Playing Fields

In addition to mown fields that are ideal for football, baseball, corn-hole boards, or sledding, the round bales, stacked one right against another in long rows—the first row almost touching the second—create a long outdoor court for other sports. Freeze tag, touch football, keep-away—the kids are always inventing some new game or variation that combines elements of gymnastics, track, ball playing, and wrestling. Some years, the family has some of the round bales wrapped in plastic. But most often, the bound and dried grasses create a cushy, serpentine runway that borders the driveway adjacent to the house.

**Chase:** When you see hay bales wrapped up in white plastic, that's called wet wrap. Farmers do that to keep in the hay's moisture so it ferments. And it becomes what's called silage.

**Dad:** We've paid someone to come do that with our round bales. You do that when your hay is wet. It will rot unless you wrap it. Fermenting is different from rotting—it makes silage, which is a nutritious, delicious feed.

**Chase:** But Caleb and I didn't know that the first time our bales were wrapped. We didn't know they have to be sealed tightly so no air can get to the wet hay. Anyway, soon after the bales were wrapped, we were up on them stabbing the taut plastic with sticks. Each time we poked the bale, it let out this farting sound. It was hysterical—or so we thought. As soon as Dad came home, we yelled to him, "Dad, you have to come out and hear this!"

He heard it all right. And then we heard him: "Those air holes will spoil the hay! You go patch every hole right this minute."

**Mom:** It was a short-lived game. So, for much of the fall and winter, we had all these perfectly white bales with something like two hundred strips of silver duct tape shining all over them.

**Dad:** It's pretty expensive to have the bales wrapped; we've been able to dry out our hay before making the round bales in the last few years.

**Ali:** My favorite thing about having dogs in the country is the game we play where you run on the hay bales and try not to let Angus catch you. He loves to play with a football, so we call him and then grab his football and run before he can get to you or to the person you throw the ball to. It's like football, but Angus is the only one on the other team, even though his best friend is Bo, and they always play around.

**Grey:** Angus can hop right up onto the hay bales. (We have to scale up the side!) He takes one bound, and then he grabs with his feet and he's on top. The new Angus is still only a puppy, but he loves running with us.

**Cayne:** He's more playful than the last Angus, who wanted to be working more than playing, I think. Even though they were both border collie puppies, every dog is different.

**Chase:** Like every cow is different, though they're all Angus cows. Like every season here on the farm is different, even though they're the same four coming around and around again.

# Final Numbers for the Year

**30 cows**—remaining animals in the Bennett herd (Most are now pregnant.)

**500,000 calves**—approximate number of calves born in Ohio this year

**500 pounds**—amount of beef stored in the Bennetts' downstairs chest freezer

**70 to 90 pounds**—amount of deer meat stored in the Bennetts' freezer

**15 egg-layers**—chickens living in the Bennett chicken coop

**31 million egg-layers**—chickens in all of Ohio, housed at approximately 4,500 farms

**120 hours**—time Caleb spent coaching his little brothers in baseball, wrestling, and football

**27 novels**—books Chase read beyond required reading for school

**154 innings**—about how much baseball Grey has played

**40 matches**—total amount Cayne wrestled (not counting practices)

**17 jigsaw puzzles and 10 coloring books**—number Ali completed

**1,400 miles**—Caleb's pretty good guess as to how many miles he or the other men drove their tractors, skid steer, and balers ("We put about 400 hours on the machines, and they probably average 3.5 miles per hour.")

**20,000 miles**—distance the family's three drivers drove the cars (The majority of those miles were within Perry County.)

**About 2.1 million farms**—number of working farms in the United States (Roughly 76,000 of those are located in Ohio, and close to a third of those raise cattle.)

**1.6 million tons**—dry weight of all the alfalfa hay harvested in Ohio (More than one million tons of other hays were also harvested.)

**22 million**—people worked in farming this year (It is often said that agriculture is the nation's largest employer.)

**If the Bennetts drove their cars at an average speed of 50 miles per hour during the year, those 20,000 miles would also equal 400 hours. They spent the same amount of time in the seat of a car as in the seat of a farm machine.**

## A Really Good Year, Really

It's the small differences—among dogs, chickens, cows, or seasons—that the Bennetts and every other farm family learn to identify and appreciate. Farming may be a science, but it's also an art that engages a family's senses, memories, emotions, and hopes. It's a mixture of both the expected and the unexpected that makes the work rewarding and exhausting, a familiar routine and a fresh challenge. "This one was a really good year—really!" Ali declares. And the rest of the family nods in agreement.

# Jumping In… Both Feet First

**As the last pages of *Our Farm* are being designed, I think back to the first days I spent on my neighbors' farm. This is early January 2006 . . .**

Chase greets me at my car and offers to conduct me on a tour of the farm. I haven't exactly dressed for the occasion, figuring that I'd be typing on my laptop at the kitchen table, and I'm wearing suede street shoes. Chase starts us out in the barn. He explains why only a few of the cows have horns, describes machinery I've never heard of, and points out the two loose roosters who "are pretty mean." I try to take it all in, as well as follow his lead . . .

over the manure piles,

left of the tractor's deep furrows,

across the iced-over puddles,

between the top two wires of the electric fence.

I have a tentative look on my face, I know, not because I'm afraid—my years of summer camp frequently included barns, with horses—but because I'm watching each footstep as we enter a corral where a dozen cows gather at a round bale.

Chase identifies the oldest cow . . . the bull . . . the red friendly cow . . . and just as we approach the gate that opens onto the lawn, both of my shoes crush through the frozen crust into an ankle-deep slush of mud and manure.

At that very instant, Chase calls, "Oh, it's really muddy here, stay over—" and turns to finish his sentence. "Should have mentioned that sooner, huh?"

"Next time . . . ," I agree, feeling the heavy sludge fill my shoes.

Needless to say, I wore boots on all my other visits, yet there were many other ways I continued to feel on less-than-firm ground, to feel less sure of myself and of what I believed.

For example, just last week, Caleb asked if he could bow-hunt for deer on the old farm where I live: a hundred acres with a pond, a few acres to mow, some gardens, and thousands of pine trees that were planted in the early 1960s as part of an Ohio reforestation project. Every year, the answer had been "sorry, no," but now the deer so overrun our property—breaking the new fruit trees, devouring the shrubs and perennials—that I gave him permission and tried not to think about it again.

Coming back from three hours of seeing dozens of deer (but none within firing range), Caleb stopped in to tell me that he had spotted coyotes. "Five coyotes. If I see them again, want me to take them out?" he asked.

Now, I gather that coyotes are a problem, even though I've never seen one here. Some quick Web research revealed that coyotes—a species of omnivorous wild dogs not native to the state—are arriving in increasing numbers. I've never heard a single account of how coyotes are a wonderful addition to your ecosystem.

I thought about my own dogs and cats and the rest of the wildlife on my property (all of which are featured on a coyote's menu). After a few days, while fact checking a few things with Caleb, I told him, "About the coyotes . . . yes, go ahead."

That very night, our cat Slinka didn't come in after her evening circle of the house. She didn't appear when the rest of the household went to bed, or at any of the times we called her in throughout the night. In the five years that she's been with us, she's only spent the night out about a dozen times. The next morning, she wasn't at the sliding glass door that looks in on her food bowl. Spayed, fully clawed, wearing a collar with our phone number, and protected by our hundred acres, she'd never given us a reason to worry. I searched again and again, making wider and wider perimeters around the house, unable to imagine any reason for her disappearance besides coyotes. Would it have made a difference if I had welcomed Caleb to hunt them earlier?

I came to the Bennett family ready to share the seasons at their farm. I was less prepared for a year that touched so frequently on life and death—that demonstrated so clearly how the death of one creature is what enables another creature to feed or survive. "I've always wanted my kids to understand death," Dave said to me, on more than one occasion. "It's a part of life, and I don't want them to fear it."

Slinka did come back. We'll never know where she'd been: Had coyotes treed her? Were coyotes still on the property? Is there one easy answer that can weigh all the lives that hang in nature's balance?

My hope is that you've been open-minded as you've listened to the seven voices in this book, and that, like me, you've come to feel that what you understand about the world (or think you do) is less important than your capacity to understand worlds—worlds that may lie no farther than the next county.

I'm forever grateful to the Bennett family for so generously sharing their home, time, and hearts with me—and with readers everywhere who have joined us here on their farm.

**—Michael J. Rosen**
**Hopewell Springs, Ohio**

# Resources About Farm Life, Agriculture, and Wildlife

**National 4-H Headquarters** serves communities of young people with a focus on "learning by doing." Their clubs work to help members become leaders, good citizens, and positive sources of change. With 6.5 million members across the U.S., and 60 million alumni, 4-H, which began over one hundred years ago as rural youth programs, emphasizes science, technology, and healthy living. (In case you were wondering, the four Hs are head, heart, hands, health.) **www.national4-hheadquarters.gov**

**Future Farmers of America (FFA)** provides students in middle and high school with hands-on work experience for careers in many areas of agriculture. With over half a million members, the organization emphasizes leadership along with practical knowledge. **www.ffa.org**

Many divisions of the **U.S. Department of Agriculture (USDA)** address rural life, environmental issues, animal care and welfare, food and grain production, or other aspects of farming:

> Its Education and Outreach Web site for students and teachers presents resources, Web links, and information on topics including backyard conservation, nutrition, farm markets, and food safety. **www.usda.gov/wps**
>
> Its Economic Research Service is a source of information and research about issues in farming, natural resources, and rural communities. The site also has a variety of maps and charts that showcase trends or changes in many areas of rural life. **http://ers.usda.gov/Emphases/Rural**

The USDA also hosts the **Rural Information Center (RIC)** at the National Agricultural Library, which is a searchable bank of articles, featured stories, and references for rural communities. **http://ric.nal.usda.gov/nal_display/index.php**

**Sci4Kids** offers animated and interactive features on agriculture, nature, and foods in the form of quizzes, games, diagrams, links, and stories. **www.ars.usda.gov/is/kids**

Finally, the USDA has Cooperative Extension Offices located in every state, with each state supporting its own network of local offices tuned into issues most important in that region, wildlife, and environment. Staffed by experts, they provide current research and advice on topics such as pond and wildlife management, agriculture, pests, safety, and local resources. **www.csrees.usda.gov/Extension/index**

**U.S. Fish & Wildlife Service** is a conservation arm of the government, working to protect, manage, and restore the country's wildlife and their habitats. The bureau oversees wildlife refuges, wetlands, and fisheries, as well as a network of ecological stations across the country. Their Web site is filled with technical information, links, and resources. It also features a great student section with maps, short courses, videos, and a world of information about birds, endangered species, and wildflowers.
**www.fws.gov/educators/students.html**

**U.S. Poultry & Egg Association** maintains a site that includes frequently asked questions about eggs and chickens, tips on raising birds, recipes, industry statistics, and other links to other related resouces.
**www.poultryegg.org/faq/index.html**

**Youth Livestock Information** is a home page hosted by Oklahoma State University that offers links to youth-friendly sites about cattle, sheep, dairy production, and agriculture.
**www.ansi.okstate.edu/library/youth.html**

They also host **Breeds of Livestock**, an encyclopedia of cattle, goat, horse, sheep, swine, and other livestock breeds. Photographs of each animal combine with extensive descriptions of the breed's history, characteristics, and world distribution.
**www.ansi.okstate.udu/breeds**

**National Junior Angus Association** is the youth site of the American Angus Association (**www.angus.org**). It offers literature about showing, feeding, and raising cattle, and also supports the ongoing activities of the Association's young members.
**www.njaa.info/literature.html**

**National Wild Turkey Federation** is an organization committed to both the conservation of wild turkeys and the hunting of these game birds. They have two outreach sites for kids of different ages: JAKES (Juniors Acquiring Knowledge, Ethics and Sportsmanship) and Xtreme JAKES, as well as a site for educators, all of which feature informative and fun material about America's wildlife.
**www.nwtf.org/jakes/**

**Michael J. Rosen** lives with his family on an old farm situated amid one hundred forested acres in Perry County, a part of Central Ohio that forms the northern tip of the Appalachian Mountains. He grew up in Columbus, Ohio, in a home built in the middle of what had been a similar farmstead. He collected things to display in the "nature center" in the family garage and built forts and campfires in the adjacent fields. From age eleven to twenty-six, he attended, and then worked at, a nearby summer camp that featured horseback riding, sailing, canoeing and other outdoor experiences.

As an undergraduate, Michael studied ornithology and animal behavior, while imagining a career as a family practitioner. But after a short stint in medical school, he went to Columbia University to study poetry.

Since 1986, Michael has published more than three dozen books for young readers and a similar number for adults.

Michael's Web site, which contains information about forthcoming and previously published books of poetry, stories, and nonfiction, as well as his work as an author and educator in schools, features a wealth of additional photographs and follow-up materials from his two years creating *Our Farm*. Visitors are welcome at www.fidosopher.com.